BAPTISTWAY®

Adult Bible Study Guide

Jesus in the Gospel of Mark

Russell Dilday

Leroy Fenton

Brian Harbour

BAPTISTWAY PRESS®
Dallas, Texas

BAPTISTWAY PRESS® Management Team

Executive Director, Baptist General Convention of Texas: Charles Wade
Coordinator, Church Health and Growth Section: H. Lynn Eckeberger
Director, Bible Study/Discipleship Center: Dennis Parrott
Administrator, Curriculum Development Office: Bernard M. Spooner

Publishing consultant: Ross West, Positive Difference Communications
Cover and Interior Design and Production: Desktop Miracles, Inc.
Front Cover Photo: The Sea of Galilee

First edition: March 2002
ISBN: 1–931060–21–5

How to Make the Best Use of This Issue

Whether you're the teacher or a student—

1. Start early in the week before your class meets.
2. Overview the study. Look at the table of contents, read the study introduction, and read the unit introduction for the lesson you're about to study. Try to see how each lesson relates to the unit and overall study of which it is a part.
3. Use your Bible to read and consider prayerfully the Scripture passages for the lesson. (You'll see that each writer has chosen a favorite translation for each unit in this issue. You're free to use the Bible translation you prefer and compare it with the translation chosen for that unit, of course.)
4. After reading all the Scripture passages in your Bible, then read the writer's comments. The comments are intended to be an aid to your study of the Bible.
5. Read the small articles—"sidebars"—in each lesson. They are intended to provide additional, enrichment information and inspiration and to encourage thought and application.
6. Try to answer for yourself the questions included in each lesson. They're intended to encourage

further thought and application, and they can also be used in the class session itself.

If you're the teacher—

A. Do all of the things just mentioned, of course.

B. In the first session of the study, briefly overview the study by identifying with your class the date on which each lesson will be studied. Lead your class to write the date in the table of contents on page 7 and on the first page of each lesson. You might also find it helpful to make and post a chart that indicates the date on which each lesson will be studied. *Note*: This study includes a bonus lesson on Mark 13. The bonus lesson is included because of the importance of the teachings of this chapter and the need to help adults understand its meaning in context. It is included as an extra lesson rather than a numbered lesson in order to give classes the choice of when and how to study it. Classes may choose to omit another lesson, combine two lessons, or study Mark 13 in an extra class meeting.

C. You may want to get the enrichment teaching help that is provided in the *Baptist Standard* and/or on the internet. Call 214–630–4571 to begin your subscription to the *Baptist Standard*. Access the internet information by checking the *Baptist Standard* website at www.baptiststandard.com.

(Other class participants may find this information helpful, too.)

D. Get a copy of the *Teaching Guide*, which is a companion piece to these lesson comments. It contains additional Bible comments plus teaching suggestions. The teaching suggestions in the *Teaching Guide* are intended to provide practical, easy-to-use teaching suggestions that will work in your class.

E. After you've studied the Bible passage, the lesson comments, and other material, use the teaching suggestions in the *Teaching Guide* to help you develop your plan for leading your class in studying each lesson.

F. Enjoy leading your class in discovering the meaning of the Scripture passages and in applying these passages to their lives.

Jesus in the Gospel of Mark

UNIT THREE

Suffering for Us

Introducing

Jesus in the Gospel of Mark

Who is Jesus, and how shall we respond to him? That question faced the people of Jesus' day who came in contact with Jesus or heard about Jesus. Wherever Jesus went, people had to decide how to respond. Neutrality was impossible. Choices were made beside fishing boats, inside synagogues and private homes, and within the judgment halls of the chief priests and Pilate. Decisions about Jesus continued to confront people even after Jesus' death. His followers said he had risen from the dead. What could one make of that?

This same question—Who is Jesus, and how shall we respond to him?—confronted the first readers of the Gospel of Mark. The Gospel of Mark likely is the first written gospel, probably appearing some thirty-five or so years after Jesus' death and resurrection. The early Christian preachers had preached the gospel, and now Mark wrote down the message that had been proclaimed about Jesus through the decades, perhaps especially as Peter preached it.

Mark's first readers may have been facing persecution in Rome during the middle of the 60s. In such a situation, a decision had to be made about Jesus. Christians themselves had to know what kind of person and message could demand their devotion even to the point of giving their lives. As the eyewitnesses to Jesus' earthly life began to pass away, these early Christians also needed information they could share with others and so lead them to commitment to Jesus.

The question continues to face people in our own day. Who is Jesus, and how shall we respond to him? In sixteen swiftly-moving chapters, the Gospel of Mark tells the story of Jesus in a way that calls for a decision by every person. Mark's message about Jesus also provides hope and assurance that commitment—the kind of commitment that means taking up our own cross and following Jesus—is indeed worthwhile. Mark's account of Jesus also is such that reading and studying it can equip Christians to share the message with others.

Perhaps you will see Jesus in a new way as you study Mark's message about him. Perhaps you will even decide to follow Jesus more closely or for the first time when you learn more about him.

Unit One, Beginning His Ministry, consists of four lessons that focus on the early portion of Jesus' ministry according to the Gospel of Mark. The Scripture selections are from Mark 1:1—4:34. The lessons show Jesus proclaiming and living the good news of the kingdom of God, facing conflict with the religious leaders, receiving varying responses from people who heard of him, and interpreting his ministry through parables.

Unit Two, Showing His Power, focuses on Jesus' actions as recorded in Mark 4:35—8:38. These actions of Jesus further demonstrated his identity and

Additional Resources for Studying *Jesus in the Gospel of Mark*[1]

William Barclay. *The Gospel of Mark*. The Daily Study Bible. Revised edition. Philadelphia: The Westminster Press, 1975.

James A. Brooks. *Mark*. The New American Commentary. Volume 23. Nashville, Tennessee: Broadman Press, 1991.

Russell H. Dilday, editor. "Studies in Mark." *Southwestern Journal of Theology*. XXI, No. 1, Fall, 1978.

David E. Garland. *Mark*. The NIV Application Commentary. Grand Rapids, Michigan: Zondervan Publishing House, 1996.

Johnnie Godwin. *Mark*. Layman's Bible Book Commentary. Volume XVI. Nashville: Broadman Press, 1979.

William Hendriksen. *The Gospel of Mark*. Grand Rapids, Michigan: Baker Book House, 1975.

Herschel H. Hobbs. *An Exposition of the Gospel of Mark*: Grand Rapids, Michigan: Baker Book House, 1970.

William L. Lane. *The Gospel According to Mark*. The New International Commentary on the New Testament. Grand Rapids, Michigan: William B. Eerdmans Publishing Company, 1974.

Thomas C. Oden, editor. *Ancient Christian Commentary on Scripture: Mark*. Downers Grove: Intervarsity Press, 1998.

Lloyd J. Ogilvie. *Life Without Limits*: Waco, Texas: Word Books, Publisher, 1975.

Ray C. Stedman. *The Servant Who Rules*. Waco, Texas: Word Books, Publisher, 1976.

Lamar Williamson, Jr. *Mark.* Interpretation: A Bible Commentary for Teaching and Preaching. Louisville: John Knox Press, 1983.

culminated in Mark 8:27–38. Those verses focus on Jesus' call for personal decision from people, beginning with his followers, about who he is. The emphasis in the first half of Mark's Gospel on Jesus' power clarifies Jesus' identity and the nature of his ministry. This emphasis on Jesus' power also sets the context for Jesus' beginning to teach in Mark 8:31 about his suffering.

Unit Three, Suffering for Us, consists of five lessons from Mark 9—16 plus an additional lesson on Mark 13. Lesson Nine shows Jesus' teaching his disciples about service as they move nearer to Jerusalem and the cross that awaited him there. In Lesson Ten, Jesus is shown asserting his authority in various ways. Lessons Eleven, Twelve, and Thirteen deal with Jesus' giving his life, being condemned, and dying and being resurrected. The bonus lesson on Mark 13 is included because of the importance of the teachings of this chapter and the need to help adults understand its meaning in context. It is included as an extra lesson rather than a numbered lesson in order to give classes the choice of when and how to study it. Classes may choose to omit another lesson, combine two lessons, or study Mark 13 in an extra class meeting.

NOTES

1. Listing a book does not imply full agreement by the writers or BAPTISTWAY PRESS® with all of its comments.

UNIT ONE

Beginning His Ministry

As intelligent, thinking citizens of the twenty-first century, we have no problem recognizing that the same current event occurring in Washington, D.C., can be reported by different magazines—say *Newsweek, Time,* and *U.S. News and World Report*—in three totally different ways. The event is the same. Yet, as the event is reported in the three different magazines, the details and slant are not the same. Why? Because each of the writers brings to the event his or her personal bias that determines how the event is interpreted. And each magazine has it own editorial policy that determines the slant of all the articles that appear in the magazine.

Compare that reality to the four gospels in the New Testament. The comparison is not exact, of course. However, we can see that each gospel emphasizes different details of Jesus' ministry and message. For example, each of the gospel writers begins the story of Jesus at a different place. Mark begins with the preaching of John the Baptist. Jesus comes bursting onto the scene in Mark's Gospel, pronouncing the arrival of the kingdom of God. In contrast, Matthew and Luke begin with Jesus' birth, each tracing his ancestry. Yet, Matthew traces Jesus' ancestry back to David, but Luke, using a different genealogy, traces Jesus' ancestry all the way back to Adam. John, on the other hand, goes back past the preaching of John the Baptist, past the birth events in Bethlehem, past the connection with David, past even the linkage to Adam, all the way back to the dawn of time. The Gospel of John declares that as far back as we can see, Jesus was already there. Same subject. Same events. But what different stories.

Why the differences? The authors of these gospels were four different individuals. They looked at Jesus from different perspectives. They were writing with different purposes. They were addressing different historical circumstances. These differences do not undermine the inspiration of the Bible. They simply confirm the richness of the content of God's word and the complexity of the process by which God brought his word to us.

In the four lessons in this unit, Mark jumps immediately into the story of Jesus' ministry without providing much background. Instead, we see immediately the broad brush strokes of Jesus' overall ministry: the power of his teaching and example (Lesson One); his conflict with the religious leaders (Lesson Two); the varying responses of the people (Lesson Three); and his use of parables to teach about the kingdom of God (Lesson Four).

Unit 1: Beginning His Ministry

UNIT ONE, BEGINNING HIS MINISTRY

Lesson 1	Jesus Proclaims and Lives the Good News	Mark 1:9–15, 29–39
Lesson 2	Jesus Faces Conflict	Mark 2:1–17; 3:1–6
Lesson 3	Jesus Encounters Varying Responses	Mark 3:7–35
Lesson 4	Jesus Interprets His Ministry	Mark 4:1–20

LESSON ONE

Jesus Proclaims and Lives the Good News

Focal Text

Mark 1:9–15, 29–39

Background

Mark 1:1–45

Main Idea

Jesus, God's Son, proclaimed the good news that the kingdom of God had now drawn near and demonstrated that reality in his life and ministry.

Question to Explore

What does Jesus' coming mean?

Study Aim

To describe the unique significance of who Jesus is and what he did

Study and Action Emphases

- Share the gospel of Jesus Christ with all people
- Minister to human needs in the name of Jesus Christ
- Equip people for ministry in the church and in the world
- Strengthen existing churches and start new congregations

Quick Read

After his baptism, Jesus announced the coming of the kingdom of God and inaugurated his ministry of preaching and healing.

I'll never forget my visit with the young couple in my office. They had attended worship for the first time at our church the previous Sunday and had asked for an appointment. The young man was the son of a minister. The young woman had been completely sheltered from any kind of religious instruction. They had been married only a few months, had recently moved to Dallas, and had visited our church the Sunday before.

Early into the conversation, I sensed an eagerness to hear about the gospel message. So I began a brief review of the life of Jesus—his birth, his teaching, his importance, and his death on the cross. I was ready to explain the resurrection when the young woman interrupted with a question: "Is there a place where all of this is written down?"

My jaw dropped, but I recovered quickly with the response, "Yes, of course. It is written in the Bible." I opened my Bible to the table of contents and explained to her that four different individuals told the story of Jesus. Each individual told the story differently, but all agreed on the basic outline of his life. I looked up and apologized, "I'm sorry. I probably shouldn't be so elementary in my explanation."

The young woman responded, "Oh, I want you to be elementary. I don't have a clue about what you are saying!"

For those of us raised in the church, the absence of any knowledge of Jesus and the Bible is somewhat disconcerting. Where does a person turn to learn about Jesus' ministry? Mark's Gospel provides a concise, straightforward retelling of the story. He began his gospel in the wilderness where John the Baptist was preaching. Suddenly, Jesus appeared on the scene and the spotlight shifted to him. In these opening verses, Jesus inaugurated his ministry.

The Preparation for His Ministry (1:9–13)

Our text begins with the phrase: "at that time" (1:9). At what time? At the time when thousands of Jews were streaming out into the wilderness to hear John preach. At the time when the waters of the Jordan were being constantly stirred as John baptized one person after another. At the time when John's ministry was at its height. At that time, Jesus appeared in the wilderness and "was baptized by John in the Jordan" (1:9).

Why did Jesus choose to be baptized?

- Perhaps Jesus was identifying with humanity. In everything he did, Jesus identified with humanity. So it was at the beginning of his ministry. Jesus was baptized to signify his solemn resolution to take upon himself the guilt of those for whom he was going to die.
- Or maybe Jesus wanted to identify with John's message. John stood at the end of the old covenant. Jesus stood at the beginning of the new covenant. What John proclaimed, Jesus would now fulfill. Thus, Jesus' baptism acknowledged his identification with the message of John.

Mark 1:9–15, 29–39

9 At that time Jesus came from Nazareth in Galilee and was baptized by John in the Jordan. 10 As Jesus was coming up out of the water, he saw heaven being torn open and the Spirit descending on him like a dove. 11 And a voice came from heaven: "You are my Son, whom I love; with you I am well pleased."

12 At once the Spirit sent him out into the desert, 13 and he was in the desert forty days, being tempted by Satan. He was with the wild animals, and angels attended him.

14 After John was put in prison, Jesus went into Galilee, proclaiming the good news of God. 15 "The time has come," he said. "The kingdom of God is near. Repent and believe the good news!"

● ●

29 As soon as they left the synagogue, they went with James and John to the home of Simon and Andrew. 30 Simon's mother-in-law was in bed with a fever, and they told Jesus about her. 31 So he went to her, took her hand and helped her up. The fever left her and she began to wait on them.

32 That evening after sunset the people brought to Jesus all the sick and demon-possessed. 33 The whole town gathered at the door, 34 and Jesus healed many who had various diseases. He also drove out many demons, but he would not let the demons speak because they knew who he was.

35 Very early in the morning, while it was still dark, Jesus
got up, left the house and went off to a solitary place,
where he prayed. 36 Simon and his companions went to
look for him, 37 and when they found him, they
exclaimed: "Everyone is looking for you!"
38 Jesus replied, "Let us go somewhere else—to the
nearby villages—so I can preach there also. That is why I
have come." 39 So he traveled throughout Galilee, preach-
ing in their synagogues and driving out demons.

- Some have suggested that Jesus was baptized in order to provide an example for us to emulate. When Jesus later instructed the church to baptize those who believed in him (Matthew 28:19–20), the church could point back to Jesus' baptism as a pattern to be followed.
- Others suggest that Jesus was baptized in order to depict the nature of his ministry—one of death and resurrection.
- The incident that followed Jesus' baptism suggests that his baptism provided an opportunity for God to affirm him.

An epiphany and an audible word penetrated the desert sky that day as Jesus was baptized. Mark gives no indication that anyone other than Jesus saw the epiphany or heard the voice. But Jesus obviously saw and heard. And the Spirit that descended on him in the form of a dove and the voice of God that reverberated through the wilderness reminded Jesus who he was. "You are my Son, whom I love," God declared, "with you I am well pleased" (1:11). This word from God affirmed Jesus in his ministry.

Jesus faced a period of temptation after his baptism by John, his anointment by the Holy Spirit, and his affirmation by God's announcement. The necessity for Jesus to face temptation is difficult for us to understand. To add to the complexity, Mark tells us "the Spirit sent him out into the desert" (1:12). Why did the Spirit send Jesus (the Greek word literally suggests that the Spirit drove Jesus out) into the wilderness? Behind Jesus' confrontation with Satan in the wilderness was the purpose of God. This is why Jesus came, to face the principalities and powers and to win victory over them. So, immediately after Jesus was identified as the one who would fulfill the purpose of God, the Spirit ushered Jesus into the arena in which that purpose would be fulfilled.

For forty days Jesus was tempted in the desert by Satan and attended by the angels. The word "tempt" originally meant to discover what good or evil was in a person, but it eventually carried the meaning of enticing a person to do evil. So for forty days, Satan tried to entice Jesus to do evil. However, Jesus resisted the temptation to take the easy way out at the beginning of his ministry as he would again on the cross at the end of his ministry.

Baptized by John, anointed by the Spirit, affirmed by God, and victorious over Satan—Jesus was prepared to inaugurate his ministry.

The Inauguration of His Ministry (1:14–15)

How did Jesus inaugurate his ministry? He proclaimed the good news of God. Jesus did not pronounce a word of condemnation, first of all, but a word of hope. He preached the good news of God. The gospel of God is the good news of hope (Colossians 1:23), the good news of peace (Ephesians 6:15), and the good news of eternal life (John 3:16). However, this hope, peace, and life were tied up with the concept of the kingdom of God. Jesus announced that the kingdom of God—the sovereign reign of God over all the earth—would begin to assert itself in human life.

Where does a person turn to learn about Jesus' ministry?

Two responses are required of us for inclusion in the kingdom of God. First, we must repent. The word literally means to change our mind, to move in a different direction. Billy Sunday (1862–1935) was a former major league baseball player who was a colorful evangelist during the early twentieth century. The story is that he would demonstrate repentance by doing a back flip as he walked one direction across the platform and then he would walk in the other direction. That is repentance. Second, we must believe. Belief is the flip side of repentance. Repentance means to recognize the evil of our sin; belief means to recognize the

"Is there a place where all of this is written down?"

goodness of Christ. Repentance means to turn from our sin; belief means to turn to Christ. Through repentance and belief, we can become a part of the kingdom of God, the sovereign reign of God on earth.

With the proclamation of the gospel of God and the announcement of the kingdom of God, Jesus inaugurated his ministry.

Messiah and Suffering Servant

The voice from heaven in Mark 1:11, "You are my Son, whom I love; with you I am well pleased," combines two different prophetic strands from the Old Testament. The first phrase is a quote from Psalm 2:7, a passage traditionally identified in Jewish eschatology with the Messiah. The second phrase, from Isaiah 42:1, refers to the Suffering Servant who would suffer vicariously for sinful humanity.

"Messiah" and "Suffering Servant" were not commonly connected at that point in history. Messianic expectations revolved around the concept of David and a restored king on the throne of Israel. However, by the time Jesus died on Calvary's cross, these two concepts—Messiah and Suffering Servant—would be irrevocably welded together. Jesus was indeed the Messiah, but not the Messiah of popular expectations. Instead, Jesus would fulfill his messianic mission, not by winning a military victory, but in victorious suffering. This statement from God in Mark 1:11 not only affirmed Jesus; it also described the nature of Jesus' ministry.

The Power of His Ministry (1:29–34)

Jesus' ministry was not just a ministry of proclamation, however. It was also a ministry of power, a power that stirred up the spirit world and startled the multitudes with its dramatic effect. By his power Jesus confounded the religious leaders. By his power Jesus calmed storms on the Sea of Galilee. By his power Jesus inspired loyalty. And by his power Jesus healed the sick.

Baptized by John, anointed by the Spirit, affirmed by God, and victorious over Satan—Jesus was prepared to inaugurate his ministry.

Peter was a benefactor of one of Jesus' earliest healings. When James and John accompanied Jesus to the home of Peter and Andrew, they discovered that Peter's mother-in-law was in bed with a serious illness. Jesus' compassion compelled him to respond to this need.

Notice the woman's response after her healing. Mark tells us "she began to wait on them" (1:31). What a beautiful picture of the response all of us should make to the healing touches of Jesus in our lives. The response to the ministry of Jesus should always be service. Or, to express it another way, Jesus saves us *for* something. That something is service.

Word spread quickly through the village so that others soon brought their sick to Jesus to be healed. The action began "that evening after sunset" (1:32). This delay does not reflect a required time sequence

Can You Hear God?

A businessperson was complaining one night about a particularly tough problem at work. His sister asked, "Have you prayed about it?"

The businessperson responded, "Whenever I can," explaining that he did most of his praying on the run. He excused his prayer pattern with the comment, "The Lord can hear me just as well when I'm running."

His sister responded, "Yes, but can *you* hear him?"

Do you have a time and place where you can be alone with God, not only to speak to him but also to listen to him speak to you?

---

before the word of the healing could get out. This was the Sabbath day (1:21), and a person could travel only so far on the Sabbath. So the crowd waited until the sun went down, indicating the Sabbath was over, and then they brought their sick to Jesus.

Jesus "healed many" and "also drove out many demons" (1:34). We see in this statement the compassion of Jesus. We also see the power of Jesus. Neither illness nor demons could resist the power of the Great Physician. Although healing was not Jesus' primary purpose, Jesus nevertheless demonstrated his healing power throughout his ministry.

Jesus' response to the demons perplexes us. Luke clearly states in his parallel account what Mark implies here: the demons knew who Jesus was and were loudly proclaiming, "You are the Son of God" (Luke 4:41). Why did they say that? Perhaps they had an irresistible fascination with Jesus. They would not accept him as their Master, and yet they knew who he was. Or perhaps they had an irrepressible desire to get Jesus in trouble. They knew that if the crowds began to proclaim Jesus as the Son of God, the religious leaders would immediately rally against him. The latter is probably correct, and this explains why Mark concludes, "he would not let the demons speak" (Mark 1:34).

Neither illness nor demons could resist the power of the Great Physician.

Jesus came preaching. And yet, in addition to preaching the good news he manifested the good news in the practical ministry of healing.

The Purpose of His Ministry (1:35–39)

Much had already transpired on that particular Sabbath. Jesus had gone to Capernaum to worship. He had been asked to teach the Bible lesson, and the response of the people was overwhelming. Then, a man interrupted the synagogue worship, and so Jesus healed him. Jesus and his disciples went to Peter's house where again Jesus was confronted by a physical need that he met. When the sun went down, people from all over the city brought their sick to Jesus, and

Jesus healed many of them. What a day it had been. After a day like that, we often feel the need to rest, and so we sleep in. Mark tells us that after this long, strenuous day, Jesus felt the need to pray. So, "very early in the morning, while it was still dark, Jesus got up, left the house and went off to a solitary place, where he prayed" (1:35).

Notice the *time* of Jesus' prayer. Jesus felt the need to begin the day with prayer (1:35). Why? Because the whole day was ahead of him, and this time with the Father in the early morning hours prepared him spiritually for all of the opportunities of the day.

Notice also the *place* of Jesus' prayer. Jesus "went off to a solitary place" (1:35). Every Christian I have ever known who had a powerful prayer life emphasized the need for a special place for prayer. A personal relationship with God cannot be developed in a crowd. To develop this intimate relationship with God demands a private place where we can meet God alone. Early in the morning, while it was still dark, Jesus went off to a solitary place where he poured out his heart to God.

Repentance means to turn from our sin; belief means to turn to Christ.

However, the appearance of Peter and some of the other disciples interrupted Jesus' private prayer. They reminded him that a crowd of people was waiting for him to minister to them. *You can do the same thing you did yesterday*, they might have said. *Your popularity will increase and much human need can be met.*

In contrast, Jesus suggested they go somewhere else instead of going back to Capernaum and that he focus on preaching the good news of the kingdom rather than spending another day healing the sick. Jesus reflected both his independence and his compassion. We see first his independence. The disciples were not going to call the shots for him. Jesus had his own agenda. He was not on a human agenda but on God's agenda. We also see Jesus' compassion. The world was bigger than Capernaum. Others had needs. Others needed to hear the good news of God. Jesus wanted to broaden the arena of his ministry.

To develop this intimate relationship with God demands a private place where we can meet God alone.

Perhaps Jesus' primary concern was not to reflect his independence or his compassion but to acknowledge his purpose. He wanted to go to other villages to preach because, he explained, "that is why I have come" (1:38). Jesus would continue to perform miracles of healing, but he never meant the miracles to be central. The focus was on his message—the good news of the kingdom of God. Jesus' purpose was to proclaim to the world the good news of God's love.

Mark reflects on the method of Jesus in the final verse of our text. As he traveled through Galilee, Mark tells us, Jesus was "preaching in their synagogues" (1:39). The origin of the synagogue, which was central to the practice of the Hebrew faith in

New Testament times, is cloaked in mystery. The synagogue developed sometime during the days of Babylonian captivity. The synagogue provided a place for worship, education, fellowship, and service in the first century world. Further, anyone who was considered suitable by the ruler of the synagogue was allowed to speak. That Jesus took advantage of this opportunity repeatedly is abundantly clear in the gospels.

Behind Jesus' confrontation with Satan in the wilderness was the purpose of God.

Implications for Us

Most of us have heard the story of Jesus so often that we miss the far-reaching implications of the gospel stories. If Jesus is indeed the Messiah who fulfilled all of the promises of God to Israel, if Jesus is indeed the unique Son of God who came to earth to establish the kingdom of God, if Jesus can transform our darkness into light and death into life, then we need to come to him again so that he can touch our lives with his power. And, we need to tell others about him so that they might know the life that is eternal that comes only through Jesus, our Savior.

QUESTIONS

1. How did Jesus' baptism and experience in the wilderness prepare him for his ministry?

2. In what ways can we prepare ourselves for our ministry today?

3. What do we learn about temptation from Jesus' experience in the wilderness?

4. What do we learn about prayer from the example of Jesus?

5. How can we reproduce Jesus' ministry of preaching and healing in the church today?

LESSON TWO

Jesus Faces Conflict

Focal Text

Mark 2:1–17; 3:1–6

Background

Mark 2:1—3:6

Main Idea

Jesus' challenge of religious tradition brought severe conflict with the religious leaders.

Question to Explore

What thoughts, actions, and traditions of ours conflict with who Jesus is and what he did?

Study Aim

To identify current counterparts to the various conflicts Jesus faced in the focal text

Study and Action Emphases

- Share the gospel of Jesus Christ with all people
- Minister to human needs in the name of Jesus Christ
- Equip people for ministry in the church and in the world

Quick Read

When Jesus offered forgiveness, healed a man on the Sabbath, and called a tax collector to be his disciple, the conflict intensified with the local religious leaders.

A church I once served began using a "blended" worship service more than twenty years ago. From time to time our minister of music would inject a more contemporary piece of music, often accompanied by a guitar and the drums. Most of our members were comfortable with this approach, except for one man in his sixties. Each Sunday he entered the sanctuary from the back and slowly walked down the right aisle to his seat on the second row. However, if he spotted the drums beside the piano as he entered the sanctuary, he would simply keep walking past his seat, out the side door, into his car, and head back home. He was wedded to a certain style of music and was unwilling to change.

Unwillingness to change is what transforms a routine into a rut and a tradition into traditionalism. Jesus confronted a similar problem as he sought to establish the kingdom of God. The "traditions" of the religious establishment conflicted with the principles of the kingdom. Consequently, instead of supporting Jesus, the religious leaders opposed him. The three incidents in our text reflect a growing conflict between Jesus and the religious establishment.

Healing the Lame Man (2:1–12)

After a period of preaching and ministering in Galilee, Jesus returned to Capernaum. Mark called Capernaum "home." In what sense was Capernaum

Mark 2:1–17

1 A few days later, when Jesus again entered Caper-
naum, the people heard that he had come home. 2 So
many gathered that there was no room left, not even
outside the door, and he preached the word to them.
3 Some men came, bringing to him a paralytic, carried by
four of them. 4 Since they could not get him to Jesus
because of the crowd, they made an opening in the roof
above Jesus and, after digging through it, lowered the
mat the paralyzed man was lying on. 5 When Jesus saw
their faith, he said to the paralytic, "Son, your sins are
forgiven."

6 Now some teachers of the law were sitting there,
thinking to themselves, 7 "Why does this fellow talk like
that? He's blaspheming! Who can forgive sins but God
alone?"

8 Immediately Jesus knew in his spirit that this was what
they were thinking in their hearts, and he said to them,
"Why are you thinking these things? 9 Which is easier: to
say to the paralytic, 'Your sins are forgiven,' or to say,
'Get up, take your mat and walk'? 10 But that you may
know that the Son of Man has authority on earth to for-
give sins. . . ." He said to the paralytic, 11 "I tell you, get
up, take your mat and go home." 12 He got up, took his
mat and walked out in full view of them all. This amazed
everyone and they praised God, saying, "We have never
seen anything like this!"

13Once again Jesus went out beside the lake. A large
crowd came to him, and he began to teach them. 14As he
walked along, he saw Levi son of Alphaeus sitting at the
tax collector's booth. "Follow me," Jesus told him, and
Levi got up and followed him.

15While Jesus was having dinner at Levi's house, many
tax collectors and "sinners" were eating with him and his
disciples, for there were many who followed him. 16When
the teachers of the law who were Pharisees saw him eat-
ing with the "sinners" and tax collectors, they asked his
disciples: "Why does he eat with tax collectors and 'sin-
ners'?"

17On hearing this, Jesus said to them, "It is not the
healthy who need a doctor, but the sick. I have not come
to call the righteous, but sinners."

Mark 3:1–6

1Another time he went into the synagogue, and a man
with a shriveled hand was there. 2Some of them were
looking for a reason to accuse Jesus, so they watched
him closely to see if he would heal him on the Sabbath.
3Jesus said to the man with the shriveled hand, "Stand up
in front of everyone."

4Then Jesus asked them, "Which is lawful on the Sab-
bath: to do good or to do evil, to save life or to kill?" But
they remained silent.

5He looked around at them in anger and, deeply dis-
tressed at their stubborn hearts, said to the man,

"Stretch out your hand." He stretched it out, and his hand was completely restored. [6]Then the Pharisees went out and began to plot with the Herodians how they might kill Jesus.

"home" to Jesus? Some suggest that Peter's home in Capernaum became the headquarters for Jesus' ministry. Therefore, whenever Jesus was there, he was "home." Others suggest a supporter of Jesus provided a place for him to stay while he was in Capernaum. More than likely, "home" means Galilee where Jesus had grown up.

Jesus' growing popularity attracted a crowd of people. The disciples, who sought to learn from and be blessed by Jesus, were a part of the crowd. The curious, those in every generation who are drawn to the famous and the powerful, also were a part of the crowd. The needy, those for whom Jesus' presence created hope and expectancy, were a part of the crowd. In addition, the critics, representatives of the religious establishment who already were nervous about this popular rabbi from Galilee, were a part of the crowd. Jesus' primary concern was not to heal but to preach, and so Mark tells us Jesus "preached the word to them" (2:2). This "word" was the word of God's love, the word of God's forgiveness, the word of God's hope.

Jesus' discussion with the multitude was interrupted by four men who lowered their friend to Jesus through an opening they had created by digging through the roof. Mark gives no record of conversation from either the man on the mat or his friends peeping into the room from above. The situation spoke for itself. Here was a person in need. Here were four friends deeply concerned about him. The five together were convinced that Jesus could do something about his problem. The entire account is punctuated with expectancy and faith.

In the Greek construction of the sentence, the first word out of Jesus' mouth after his greeting to the paralyzed man was the offer of forgiveness. "Forgiven are your sins," Jesus said to the man on the mat (2:5, author's translation). Why did Jesus say that? Why not just tell him to get up and walk? Jesus himself answered that question (2:9–10). Let me paraphrase Jesus' response: "Two things are difficult for a person to do: to forgive a person and to heal a person from lameness. I have the authority to do both. I will prove the one you cannot see by the one you can see." The critics in the crowd could see the crippled man stand up and walk; they could not see the man forgiven. But Jesus provided the outward demonstration of the one to prove the reality of both.

Unwillingness to change is what transforms a routine into a rut and a tradition into traditionalism.

In their response to Jesus, the critics were right in their premise but wrong in their conclusion. Their premise, "Who can forgive sins but God alone?" (2:7), is accurate. Only God can forgive. However, the conclusion they reached from that premise was incorrect. If Jesus claimed to do something only God could do, then Jesus was either divine or an imposter. Jesus' critics chose the latter conclusion, missing the clear signal about who Jesus was.

Ironically, Jesus immediately proved their conclusion wrong. They refused to believe he was divine. Jesus immediately displayed his divine perception by discerning what they were thinking (2:8). He also displayed his divine power by healing the paralytic (2:10–11). Having entered the room as a cripple, this man exited with his pallet tucked under his arm, moving in his own strength.

Mark contrasts the response of the multitude with the response of the religious leaders. The religious leaders stood back, skeptical and suspicious, but the rest of the people were amazed and grateful. "We have never seen anything like this!" they exclaimed (2:12).

Calling Levi (2:13–17)

The scene changes, from a stuffy crowded room to the fresh air of a pastoral lakeside setting. Again, a crowd gathered around Jesus as he walked along the path beside the lake. Following a common pattern of that day, Jesus taught them as he walked along. The traveling classroom was halted by an encounter with a tax collector, sitting at his desk. Mark identifies this tax collector as Levi. In the gospel the tax collector later wrote, this tax collector turned disciple called himself Matthew (Matthew 9:9).

The key to this incident, however, was not the man's name but his profession. Levi was a tax collector, a member of the network of people set up to collect the revenues for the Roman government. The Jews of Jesus' day labeled the tax collectors with three words: traitor, extortionist, and outcast.

The Sabbath

The word *sabbath* comes from a Hebrew word meaning "to cease." The Ten Commandments cite the Sabbath as a day that belongs to the Lord. It is considered a day of rest, for two reasons: (1) God rested on the seventh day after creation (Exodus 20:8–11); and (2) the Sabbath serves as a reminder of Israel's deliverance from Egyptian slavery (Deuteronomy 5:12–15).

In the Old Testament period, the Sabbath was considered a day for worship and rest. During the inter-biblical period, additional restrictions were connected with the Sabbath.

Jesus observed the Sabbath as a day of worship. However, he disregarded the restrictions commonly held by the religious leaders of his day. He plucked grain from the field, an activity considered harvesting and thus restricted on the Sabbath (Mark 2:23–24). He healed the sick, an activity considered work and thus restricted on the Sabbath (Luke 13:10–14). Jesus told the religious leaders, "The Son of Man is Lord of the Sabbath" (Matt. 12:8).

The tax collectors turned their backs on their fellow citizens and served the foreign oppressor, Rome. Since no systematic plan existed for the collection of these taxes, the local collectors usually abused the system to accumulate personal wealth. Consequently, these tax collectors were rejected by society. Their title was often attached to the word "sinners" as a label for anyone who was indecent, uncommitted, and reproachable in society. Levi was a tax collector. Jesus' invitation to Levi to be his disciple was therefore a clear challenge to the cultural standards of the day.

> *The five together were convinced that Jesus could do something about his problem.*

Levi's response to Jesus was immediate and permanent. In response to Jesus' invitation, "Levi got up and followed him" (Mark 2:14). The permanence of Levi's commitment is reflected more clearly in Luke's Gospel. Describing the response of Levi to Jesus' call, Luke tells us: "Levi got up, left everything and followed him" (Luke 5:28). The fishermen disciples—James and John, Peter and Andrew—could return to their trade if things did not work out with Jesus. In fact, they did just that after the crucifixion (John 21). However, Levi could not return to his trade. Once he left the lucrative position of tax collector, he would be immediately replaced, and his opportunity would be gone forever. His commitment to Jesus was therefore complete and permanent.

The nature of Levi's response is most clearly seen in the banquet he provided for Jesus and his friends (Mark 2:15). By providing the banquet, Levi displayed the honor he wanted to give Jesus. Levi wanted all of his friends to meet Jesus. Levi also displayed the honor he wanted to give his friends. Levi wanted Jesus to have the opportunity to meet all his friends. What a beautiful picture of the response every believer needs to make: honoring Jesus by giving our all to him and honoring our friends by bringing them to Jesus.

What a beautiful picture of the response every believer needs to make: honoring Jesus by giving our all to him and honoring our friends by bringing them to Jesus.

Jesus' attitude of openness toward the "tax collectors and 'sinners'" contrasted sharply with the attitude of the religious establishment. These contrasting attitudes created an adversarial relationship between Jesus and "the teachers of the law who were Pharisees" (2:16).

The common code of etiquette for religious leaders was that they should not sit down to eat with the rabble, of which the "tax collectors and 'sinners'" were a part. Jesus clearly broke that rule by dining with what the religious leaders considered the rabble of society. So these religious leaders questioned the disciples of Jesus about his behavior. Why did they approach the disciples instead of Jesus? Perhaps they were not yet bold enough to confront Jesus face to face. Or, maybe, they thought the clarification to the disciples that they were breaking the religious custom would motivate them to disassociate themselves with Jesus. The disciples did not turn from Jesus, however. Rather, they reported to Jesus what the religious leaders had said.

Instead of discussing the appropriateness of the religious custom, Jesus appealed to common sense. Think of a physician, Jesus suggested. What is the physician's purpose? The purpose is to heal those who are sick. How is the physician to do that? By remaining isolated from them? By refusing to see them? By refraining from any personal contact with them? No. The physician can carry out the work of healing only by coming into personal contact with the sick.

To Jesus, meeting human need was the top priority.

Jesus identified himself as a spiritual physician. His purpose is to make people well spiritually. How could he do that? By remaining isolated from them? By refusing to see them? By refraining from any personal contact with them? No. He could only carry out his healing work by coming into personal contact with them.

Jesus contrasted the "righteous" to the "sinners" (2:17). The "righteous" are those who think themselves worthy of God; "sinners" are those who know they are not worthy of God. Jesus was saying something like this: *If a person thinks he is worthy of God, I can't do anything for him. He already has all the answers and will not listen to what I have to say. But a person*

Dealing with Criticism

Jesus teaches us three lessons about criticism in this passage.

- Jesus did not ignore the criticism. He acknowledged the criticism of the religious leaders and responded to it.
- Jesus did not, however, return criticism with criticism. Instead, he attempted to clarify the misunderstanding that led to criticism.
- Jesus did not allow the criticism to stop him. He could have kept the peace by refusing to heal the man on the Sabbath. Instead, Jesus did what was right, regardless of the consequences.

who wants more than anything else to be accepted by God but knows that he is unworthy of God's acceptance because of his sin—that is the person I can help.

Making the Man's Hand Whole (3:1–6)

The setting of the third incident in our text is an unidentified synagogue, probably still somewhere in Galilee. The man in need had "a shriveled hand" (3:1), a paralysis of some kind. Written between the lines of this story are two opposing attitudes toward human need. To the Pharisees, observing human rules was the top priority. To Jesus, meeting human need was the top priority. These contrasting attitudes inevitably led to conflict.

The conflict between Jesus and the religious leaders had moved to a deeper level, for on this occasion, the religious leaders were not merely casual observers. Instead, they were specifically "looking for a reason to accuse Jesus" (3:2). As Jesus faced the man with the paralyzed hand, he could see out of his peripheral vision the careful scrutiny of the religious leaders.

> *How important for us today to emulate the pattern of Jesus rather than perpetuating the misplaced zeal of the religious leaders.*

Jesus had two alternatives. He could have done nothing. He could have told the man with the crippled hand, *I'm sorry. I'd like to be able to help you, but, after all, Sabbath rules prohibit healing you on this day. Rules are rules.* Or, he could heal the man. He could say, *Meeting this human need is more important than following any silly rules.*

We see Jesus' choice in verse 3. Jesus chose to heal the man's useless hand so that it could become useful again. So Jesus told the man, "'Stand up in front of everyone'" (3:3). Why did Jesus say that? Perhaps Jesus wanted to exhibit clearly his response to the man in need. Or perhaps Jesus wanted to draw on the sympathy of the crowd.

In either case, Jesus used the event not only as an opportunity to heal the man but also as an opportunity to educate the religious leaders. "'Which is lawful on the Sabbath,'" he asked them, "'to do good or to do evil, to save life or to kill?'" (3:4). The answer was obvious. Yet, the religious leaders remained silent. Jesus reacted with anger and grief, anger because of the insensitivity of the religious leaders, grief at the negative impact of that insensitivity in the lives of those who had needs. And he reacted to the man in need with compassion.

Standing before Jesus was a man with a need he could meet. So Jesus healed the crippled hand and made it whole again with a healing that was instantaneous and complete.

The man whose hand was healed responded to Jesus with gratitude and thanksgiving. The crowd responded with awe and amazement. Mark does not mention either of these reactions, however, because his focus is on the religious leaders. How did they react? Mark explains, "Then the Pharisees went out and began to plot with the Herodians how they might kill Jesus" (3:6).

If Jesus claimed to do something only God could do, then Jesus was either divine or an imposter.

What an amazing reaction. Jesus had just healed a man of his physical problem. A life had been preserved. Yet, instead of rejoicing, the religious leaders left the synagogue in a huff and began to plot with the Herodians on how they might put Jesus to death. This unholy alliance formed around a desire to maintain their respective positions of power, the Herodians in the political realm, the Pharisees in the religious realm.

Implications for Us

Leaders in the church today can find some comfort in the fact that even Jesus was not given universal followship. Even Jesus was opposed when he threatened time-honored traditions. Even Jesus was criticized when he rejected the accepted patterns of the day. For Jesus, it was a matter of principle and priority. Principle was more important than tradition, and ministering to people in need took priority over following religious etiquette. How important for us today to emulate the pattern of Jesus rather than perpetuating the misplaced zeal of the religious leaders.

QUESTIONS

1. What are the implications of Jesus' claim to be able to forgive sin?

2. How can we avoid stigmatizing certain groups of peoplc today as being off limits for relationships?

3. What sacrifices have we made to follow Christ?

4. In what ways does your church give priority to rules and rituals that prevent you from ministering to the needs of people?

Focal Text

Mark 3:7–35

Background

Mark 3:7–35

Main Idea

People responded to Jesus on the basis of their willingness to do the will of God.

Question to Explore

Why do people respond in varying ways to Jesus?

LESSON THREE Jesus Encounters Varying Responses

Study Aim

To evaluate the depth and nature of my response to Jesus

Study and Action Emphases

- Share the gospel of Jesus Christ with all people
- Minister to human needs in the name of Jesus Christ
- Equip people for ministry in the church and in the world
- Develop Christian families

Quick Read

As Jesus continued his ministry, he drew a variety of responses from his friends and from his enemies. Therefore, Jesus chose twelve individuals with whom to develop a special relationship.

Is Shaquille O'Neal an extraordinarily gifted basketball player, or is he just a bully who uses his size to overpower his opponents? Is he one of the greatest players in the National Basketball Association today or does he dominate on the court simply because the officials allow him to get by with everything? Even after he led the Los Angeles Lakers to their second consecutive NBA championship and won his second consecutive Most Valuable Player award for the 2001 NBA finals, opinions are still divided on this mammoth player known simply as "Shaq." The varying opinions of his greatness are influenced by the personal knowledge a person has of him, by one's feelings about the other members of the Lakers, by the evaluation of the head coach of the Lakers, and by dozens of other factors. Public figures inevitably generate a kaleidoscope of opinions about themselves.

Jesus also generated diverse responses. Those who were close to him were becoming aware of his uniqueness. Perhaps, they speculated, he might even be the Messiah. Others saw him simply as a popular teacher to inspire them. Some were drawn to him because of his powerful miracles. Others identified him as Public Enemy Number One. We will investigate those divergent opinions in this week's lesson.

The Crowd (3:7–12)

A friend told me recently she was going to spend a week at the end of the summer at Panama City just

Mark 3:7–35

[7]Jesus withdrew with his disciples to the lake, and a large crowd from Galilee followed. [8]When they heard all he was doing, many people came to him from Judea, Jerusalem, Idumea, and the regions across the Jordan and around Tyre and Sidon. [9]Because of the crowd he told his disciples to have a small boat ready for him, to keep the people from crowding him. [10]For he had healed many, so that those with diseases were pushing forward to touch him. [11]Whenever the evil spirits saw him, they fell down before him and cried out, "You are the Son of God." [12]But he gave them strict orders not to tell who he was.

[13]Jesus went up on a mountainside and called to him those he wanted, and they came to him. [14]He appointed twelve—designating them apostles—that they might be with him and that he might send them out to preach [15]and to have authority to drive out demons. [16]These are the twelve he appointed: Simon (to whom he gave the name Peter); [17]James son of Zebedee and his brother John (to them he gave the name Boanerges, which means Sons of Thunder); [18]Andrew, Philip, Bartholomew, Matthew, Thomas, James son of Alphaeus, Thaddaeus, Simon the Zealot [19]and Judas Iscariot, who betrayed him.

[20]Then Jesus entered a house, and again a crowd gathered, so that he and his disciples were not even able to eat. [21]When his family heard about this, they went to take charge of him, for they said, "He is out of his mind."

22And the teachers of the law who came down from
Jerusalem said, "He is possessed by Beelzebub! By the
prince of demons he is driving out demons."
23So Jesus called them and spoke to them in parables:
"How can Satan drive out Satan? 24If a kingdom is
divided against itself, that kingdom cannot stand. 25If a
house is divided against itself, that house cannot stand.
26And if Satan opposes himself and is divided, he cannot
stand; his end has come. 27In fact, no one can enter a
strong man's house and carry off his possessions unless
he first ties up the strong man. Then he can rob his
house. 28I tell you the truth, all the sins and blasphemies
of men will be forgiven them. 29But whoever blasphemes
against the Holy Spirit will never be forgiven; he is guilty
of an eternal sin."
30He said this because they were saying, "He has an evil
spirit."
31Then Jesus' mother and brothers arrived. Standing
outside, they sent someone in to call him. 32A crowd was
sitting around him, and they told him, "Your mother and
brothers are outside looking for you."
33"Who are my mother and my brothers?" he asked.
34Then he looked at those seated in a circle around him
and said, "Here are my mother and my brothers! 35Who-
ever does God's will is my brother and sister and mother."

hanging out on the beach. She called it her time for healing from all the emotional drain. If anyone ever needed healing from the emotional drain, it was Jesus. Yet, as he slipped away to the seaside for a breather from his teaching and healing ministry, the crowd followed him again. They pressed so closely to him that he had a boat ready to facilitate an escape from the crowd (Mark 3:9).

Mark identifies several groups in the crowd. Some were from the south (Judea), especially around Jerusalem. Some were from even further south in Idumea. Some were from beyond the Jordan—that is, east of the Jordan in Perea. Some were from Tyre and Sidon, the area northwest of Galilee known as Phoenicia. Mark portrays in these groups an ever-widening area of influence being touched by Jesus' ministry.

Public figures inevitably generate a kaleidoscope of opinions about themselves.

Why was the crowd rushing to be with Jesus? Because word had spread that not only could Jesus heal the sick but that there was healing power even in his touch. Consequently, some who were eager to be healed did not wait for him to touch them. Instead, they crowded around him to try to touch him. The word "crowding" in 3:9 is from the Greek word that means *to press hard upon.* This same word was used to describe the process of pressing grapes so as to extract the juice. Perhaps the pressing crowd would literally crush Jesus. In light of that possibility, Jesus told his disciples to have a boat ready in case he needed it.

In addition to the crowd, Mark acknowledges the presence of "evil spirits" who testified that Jesus was "the Son of God" (3:11). Surprisingly, Jesus responded by silencing them. Mark tells us, "But he gave them strict orders not to tell who he was" (3:12). Why? Perhaps the identity of Jesus was such an exalted truth that it was not fitting for "evil spirits" to bear witness of it. Or, perhaps this is another manifestation of the "Messianic secret" in the Gospel of Mark. The idea of the "Messianic secret" refers to Jesus' hesitancy to be identified with the common terminology for the expected Messiah because it would create false images in the minds of the people about what Jesus had come to do. Maybe Jesus anticipated the accusation of the scribes from Jerusalem that Jesus was possessed by Beelzebul and that he was in alliance with demons (3:22). If Jesus let the demons advertise who he was, this would confirm their allegations. Consequently, Jesus silenced the evil spirits.

Even as the crowds flocked around him, Jesus was aware that this was not why he had come to the earth.

The Twelve (3:13–19)

Even as the crowds flocked around him, Jesus was aware that this was not why he had come to the earth. He had not come to be a popular teacher or a miracle worker. The purpose of Jesus' coming was to give his life as a ransom for many (Mark 10:45). Even at this point, Calvary loomed ever before Jesus. The work of the kingdom, inaugurated in his brief time on the

Apostles

The twelve disciples chosen by Jesus are designated as "apostles" (3:14). The term means *messenger* or *envoy*, designating those who are sent on behalf of another. An apostle was the designation given to those who witnessed the resurrected Lord and consequently proclaimed the message of that resurrected Lord to the world.

After the resurrection, the church expanded the use of the term *apostle*. The replacement for Judas not only had to be an eyewitness of the resurrected Jesus but also an eyewitness of his ministry from the days of his baptism (Acts 1:21–22). Because the term was related to a specific set of historical requirements—experience with the resurrected Lord and with his earthly ministry—the official position of apostle, by definition, died with its initial representatives.

---

earth, was to be carried forward by men and women who would become the nucleus of the church. The selection of twelve individuals to serve as his inner core was, therefore, a significant moment in Jesus' ministry.

In John 15:16, Jesus would tell the disciples, "You did not choose me, but I chose you and appointed you to go and bear fruit." What he declared in John 15, we see described in Mark 3. Jesus knew the ones who would fit into his inner core. Jesus knew the ones God could use in this unique way, and so Jesus called those whom he himself wanted.

Why did Jesus choose twelve? Probably Jesus had in mind the new Israel. As there were twelve tribes in the old Israel, there would be twelve apostles in the new Israel.

What were the disciples to do? The first commission to the disciples was to spend time in fellowship with the Master. Mark tells us, "He appointed twelve—designating them apostles—that they might be with him" (3:14). The disciples were to enjoy fellowship with Jesus. The second commission to the disciples was to proclaim the good news to the world. Jesus chose them, not only to fellowship with him, but also "that he might send them out to preach" (3:14). The second commission grows out of the first. Discipleship is not just a matter of receiving from the Master. Discipleship also includes giving to others out of the overflow of what the Master has given to us. The call to discipleship includes the commission to share the good news with others. The third commission is liberation. Jesus selected the twelve "to have authority to drive out demons" (3:15). Perhaps we can best understand this ministry of liberation in the terms Jesus used to define his own ministry. When Jesus addressed his hometown synagogue, he read from the scroll of Isaiah this passage: "The Spirit

After having spent time with the Master, and as they went out to preach the good news, the disciples were to be about the work of liberating people from the burdens and bondage of their lives.

of the Lord is on me, because he has anointed me to preach good news to the poor. He has sent me to proclaim freedom for the prisoners and recovery of sight for the blind, to release the oppressed, to proclaim the year of the Lord's favor" (Luke 4:18–19). Then, Jesus concluded, "'Today this scripture is fulfilled in your hearing'" (Luke 4:21). In other words, Jesus was saying, *This is what I have come to do: to set people free, to release them from their burdens, to lift them out of the ruts of their existence.* In our text, Jesus passed on that responsibility to the disciples. After having spent time with the Master, and as they went out to preach the good news, the disciples were to be about the work of liberating people from the burdens and bondage of their lives.

Who were the Twelve? The names of the Twelve are cited four times in Scripture—in our text, in the parallel passages (Matt. 10:2–4; Luke 6:14–16), and in Acts 1:13, 16. Peter, James, and John head Mark's list. Perhaps Mark mentioned these three first because they formed an inner circle of the inner circle who were more intimately associated with Jesus than the others.

Two lessons are clear from this story.

- First, we learn that Jesus uses all kinds of people to carry out his kingdom work. Included in the little band of disciples was Peter the optimist and Thomas the pessimist; Simon the one-time Zealot who hated the tax-demanding Romans and Matthew who collected taxes for the

Romans; Peter the bold one and Andrew who worked more comfortably behind the scenes.

- Second, we learn that the key to our usability is not our ability but our availability. These individuals chosen by Jesus were not necessarily more gifted than others. They were, however, available for the Master's service.

The Friends (3:20–21)

Among those in the group who crowded around Jesus as he returned to Capernaum were some identified by Mark as "his family" (3:21, NIV). They are identified as "his own people" in the New American Standard Bible. The King James Version identifies these people as Jesus' "friends" instead of his family. The King James Version seems to be more accurate since Mark will later say, "Then Jesus' mother and brothers arrived" (3:31). If his mother and brothers did not arrive until later, then the individuals in verse 21 must be someone else. The preferred interpretation is "friends."

. . . Jesus described family not as people to whom we are physically connected but as those to whom we are spiritually connected.

These friends wanted to take charge of Jesus, Mark tells us, saying, "'He is out of his mind'" (3:21). Why would these friends think Jesus had lost his mind? First, Jesus' confrontation of the religious leaders of the day did not seem to be a rational approach for establishing his spiritual leadership. In addition, Jesus often seemed to present mixed signals about his identity, on the one hand offering forgiveness, something only God could do, and on the other hand, eating with sinners and outcasts, something they felt God would not do. So "they went to take charge of him," Mark explains (3:21). The word behind this translation is the same Greek word Mark used to describe Herod's arrest of John the Baptist (Mark 6:17), the attempt of the religious authorities to lay hold on Jesus (Mark 12:12), and the actual arrest of Jesus (Mark 14:44, 46). With good intentions, Jesus' friends attempted to whisk Jesus away from the crowds for his physical and emotional well-being.

Disciples

The need in the church today is not just for converts but also for disciples. What does it mean to be a disciple today? Being a disciple means

- To believe in Jesus
- To spend time with Jesus
- To follow after Jesus
- To learn from Jesus
- To tell about Jesus

The Critics (3:22–30)

Among the religious leaders who came to observe Jesus, another opinion was expressed: Jesus was aligned spiritually with the Prince of Darkness himself (3:22). What did the religious leaders see when they arrived at Capernaum on their investigative assignment? They saw the crowds flocking to Jesus. They heard the crowd whispering that Jesus might be the Messiah. They saw people amazed by Jesus' remarkable power. Since they could not deny Jesus' power, the religious leaders instead attributed Jesus' power to an evil source. They insinuated, "'He is possessed by Beelzebub!'" (3:22).

The family of God is both inclusive and exclusive.

Jesus responded with a three-point sermon. First, Jesus offered a refutation to the charge in a series of parabolic statements that revealed the idiocy of the accusation (3:23–26). If Jesus, who was casting out demons and undermining the work of Satan, was sent by Satan to do these very things, then Satan's strategy was certainly flawed. Then Jesus provided an explanation (3:27). A robber does not enlist the owner of the house to help him accomplish his theft. Instead, the robber must bind the owner. Only then can the robber accomplish his work. Likewise, Jesus was not working with Satan. Instead, he was in the process of binding Satan so that he could deprive Satan of his furniture—that is, the hearts and lives of humankind.

Finally, Jesus presented an exhortation in which he reminded the religious leaders that as long as they attributed that which is of God to Satan, they would not be involved in his work of redemption and forgiveness.

The Family (3:31–35)

Jesus' friends sought to take Jesus away because they feared for his emotional welfare. Jesus' enemies sought to discredit Jesus because they were concerned about their own political welfare. In addition, Jesus' mother and brothers arrived in Capernaum (3:31). The clear implication of the New Testament is that these were children of Mary, born after Jesus (Matt. 12:46–47; Luke 8:19; John 2:12). Their motive for approaching Jesus at this point is unclear. Prevented by the crowd from getting to Jesus, they sent word to Jesus that they wanted to talk with him.

In his response, Jesus described family not as people to whom we are physically connected but as those to whom we are spiritually connected. Jesus' intention was to create a family of God, and Jesus revealed to the crowd that one's connection with that family is not determined by physical bloodlines but by spiritual commitment. His family is "whoever does God's will" (3:35).

The family of God is both inclusive and exclusive. We see the inclusiveness of the family of God in the word "whoever." Anyone—male or female, old or young, rich or poor, slave or free—can be a part of the family of God. We see the exclusiveness of the family of God in the phrase "does God's will." Anyone can be a part of the family of God, but not everyone will be—only those who choose to do the will of God.

Implications for Us

We see in this week's lesson several different ways to respond to Jesus. On the one hand, some misunderstand Jesus, mistaking him to be insane, unaware that he is the one spot of sanity in our world. Then, some reject Jesus, unconvinced that he really is from God. Others reflect a desire to relate to Jesus but want to base that relationship on a distorted view of who Jesus really is. Still others deliberately choose to do his will in their lives. Unaware, unconvinced, uninformed, or unreserved—what will your reaction be to Jesus?

Unaware, unconvinced, uninformed, or unreserved—what will your reaction be to Jesus?

QUESTIONS

1. What popular conceptions of Jesus today may not fit with the New Testament picture of him?

2. What are the practical dimensions of discipleship in today's world?

3. What are some common criticisms of Jesus and the church today?

4. In what ways do we limit the inclusiveness of the family of God?

5. What does it mean to say that the family of God is not only inclusive but also exclusive?

LESSON FOUR

Jesus Interprets His Ministry

Focal Text

Mark 4:1–20

Background

Mark 4:1–34

Main Idea

Though the reactions to Jesus vary, the harvest Jesus proclaimed is certain and abundant, with people's response to Jesus determining their place in that harvest.

Question to Explore

In light of varying views of Jesus today, how can we be assured that Jesus really is the Christ and that Christ's way will be victorious?

Study Aim

To consider my place in the coming certain victory of God's kingdom

Study and Action Emphases

- Share the gospel of Jesus Christ with all people
- Equip people for ministry in the church and in the world
- Strengthen existing churches and start new congregations

Quick Read

Using the common image of a farmer sowing his seed, Jesus provided a rich illustration of the task of evangelism.

Both of my parents spent their lives as teachers, and so I have great respect for the men and women who have given themselves to this profession. Sometimes, however, we do not appreciate teachers as we should. One child wrote to her pastor, "Dear Pastor, Please say a prayer for my teacher. She is sick and if you say a prayer she will get better and come back to school." Then she added this P.S.: "The other kids in my class said I shouldn't write this letter." Despite their shortcomings, teachers are, apart from our parents, the primary influences on our lives.

In addition to being a herald of the gospel and a healer of the sick, Jesus was also a teacher. Through parables and pictures, Jesus illuminated the kingdom of God to his first century contemporaries. One of his most enduring stories is our text for today—the parable of the sower.

The Story (4:1–9)

Again we see Jesus teaching beside the sea, and again his teaching captured the attention of the multitude. On this occasion, the size of the crowd forced Jesus to push off the shore in a boat that was transformed into a pulpit. He taught the multitude in parables, sometimes described as "earthly stories with heavenly meanings." The first of the parables Mark records in our text is the parable of the sower. This parable focused on an ordinary happening of everyday life—a

Mark 4:1–20

1Again Jesus began to teach by the lake. The crowd
that gathered around him was so large that he got into a
boat and sat in it out on the lake, while all the people
were along the shore at the water's edge. 2He taught
them many things by parables, and in his teaching said:
3"Listen! A farmer went out to sow his seed. 4As he was
scattering the seed, some fell along the path, and the
birds came and ate it up. 5Some fell on rocky places,
where it did not have much soil. It sprang up quickly,
because the soil was shallow. 6But when the sun came
up, the plants were scorched, and they withered because
they had no root. 7Other seed fell among thorns, which
grew up and choked the plants, so that they did not bear
grain. 8Still other seed fell on good soil. It came up, grew
and produced a crop, multiplying thirty, sixty, or even a
hundred times."

9Then Jesus said, "He who has ears to hear, let him hear."

10When he was alone, the Twelve and the others around
him asked him about the parables. 11He told them, "The
secret of the kingdom of God has been given to you. But
to those on the outside everything is said in parables 12so
that,

"'they may be ever seeing but never perceiving,
and ever hearing but never understanding;
otherwise they might turn and be forgiven!'"

13Then Jesus said to them, "Don't you understand this
parable? How then will you understand any parable? 14The

farmer sows the word. 15 Some people are like seed along
the path, where the word is sown. As soon as they hear it,
Satan comes and takes away the word that was sown in
them. 16 Others, like seed sown on rocky places, hear the
word and at once receive it with joy. 17 But since they have
no root, they last only a short time. When trouble or per-
secution comes because of the word, they quickly fall
away. 18 Still others, like seed sown among thorns, hear the
word; 19 but the worries of this life, the deceitfulness of
wealth and the desires for other things come in and choke
the word, making it unfruitful. 20 Others, like seed sown on
good soil, hear the word, accept it, and produce a crop—
thirty, sixty or even a hundred times what was sown."

farmer sowing seeds—but Jesus stretched the dimensions of the ordinary with extraordinary spiritual truth. What would happen to the seeds sown by the farmer? Jesus identified four possibilities.

Footpaths intertwined the field like spider webs where the farmer would walk as he sowed his seeds. This ground had not been broken up by the plow. Instead, it was hard and unreceptive. Consequently, seeds that fell on this soil did not penetrate but lay there to be snatched by birds swooping down from the sky. These seeds, of course, produced no fruit because they never had time to grow in the soil.

Much of the tillable land in Palestine was just a thin layer of soil on a bed of rock. When the seed fell on this shallow layer of soil, the seed would germinate quickly and spring up, without sending down roots.

The broiling sun would sap the plant, for the plant had no roots and consequently had no moisture to combat the heat of the sun. Seed that fell on this soil did spring up but withered before it could produce any fruit.

Other seed fell on fertile ground that was more receptive than the footpaths and deeper than the thin layer of soil that covered the underlying stones. In this soil, the seed put down its roots and sprang into life. However, alongside the plants were thorns that, being hardier, soon choked out the plants by absorbing all the water and resources from the soil. This seed gave the promise of fruit, but the plants were choked out before the fruit could be produced.

The crop was not a total failure, however, for "other seed fell on good soil" (4:8). Here, the roots took hold, drawing into the plant the resources of the soil. Here, no thorns claimed the resources of the soil. Consequently, these seeds bore fruit, "multiplying thirty, sixty, or even a hundred times" (4:8).

Jesus concluded the parable with an admonition often repeated in the gospels: "He who has ears to hear, let him hear" (4:9). We must go beyond perception to comprehension. Jesus was not talking about the kind of hearing we do with our ears but the kind of hearing we do with our hearts.

The Paradox (4:10–12)

The disciples themselves were having difficulty "hearing" what Jesus was saying. They not only wondered about the meaning of Jesus' parable. They also wondered why Jesus taught in parables. Before explaining the story to the disciples, Jesus responded to the disciples' question about his use of parables. These verses serve as a transition between the presentation of the parable and its interpretation. They also articulate a paradox that has troubled Christians across the centuries.

Jesus revealed to the disciples through his parables that God's rule in human hearts is realized in his coming.

Why did Jesus teach in parables? For one thing, Jesus' used parables to reveal to his disciples the "secret of the kingdom of God" (4:11). The Greek word translated "secret" can also be translated "mystery." In the New Testament, a mystery is not necessarily something that cannot be understood. A mystery is something that cannot be understood unless it is revealed. It is truth that would have remained unknown had God not revealed it. So Jesus told the disciples they had been given the revealed secret of the kingdom of God. What is this revealed secret? Jesus revealed to the disciples through his parables that God's rule in human hearts is realized in his coming. Jesus revealed that truth to his disciples and to all who accepted him in genuine faith.

On the other hand, Jesus used parables to hide from the outsiders "the secret of the kingdom of God." Jesus affirmed that he spoke in parables "so that 'they may be ever seeing but never perceiving'" (4:12).

What could Jesus possibly mean by that statement? Perhaps Jesus feared that some would rush too quickly into the kingdom of God without understanding the full implications of their commitment. Attracted by the glitter of the gospel, they might move toward Jesus with too much haste. Therefore, Jesus spoke in parables so that those who were simply looking for a quick fix or an easy answer to life would be put off. Unless they dug deeper, unless they looked through the eyes of faith, they would not understand what Jesus had to offer.

The parable is not about a farmer who sows seed but about a witness who sows the word.

That is just one possible interpretation of one of the most perplexing passages in the New Testament. Mark does not dwell on Jesus' paradoxical statement or expand on the response of the religious leaders. Instead, Mark zooms in on the dialogue between Jesus and his disciples.

The Explanation (4:13–20)

Of course, Jesus was not giving a discourse on farming methodology. The parable is not about a farmer who sows seed but about a witness who sows the word. The farmer is a model of how we are to sow the word of God in the world and how different people will respond to our effort. This is the work of evangelism—sowing the word of God in the world. Jesus clearly identified three elements of evangelism.

First, evangelism requires a messenger, and so Jesus said in verse 14: "'The farmer sows the word.'" The farmer is not identified in this parable. However, in the parable of the tares in Matthew 13:37, Jesus identified the sower as the Son of Man. That is, in that parable, the sower is Jesus himself. Yet, I believe we can legitimately conclude that, in this parable, the

Parable

The word "parable" comes from two Greek words, *para*, which means "beside," and *ballo*, which means "to cast." A parable is thus a story thrown down beside some truth to illustrate it. Only Jesus in the New Testament used the parable as a teaching form. In fact, during a period in his ministry Jesus used this teaching form exclusively as he taught the multitudes (Matt. 13:34).

Some try to distinguish the parable from the allegory by pointing out that a parable has only one central meaning while, in an allegory, each part of the story has a particular meaning. However, many of Jesus' parables contain the typical characteristics of an allegory so that it is more accurate to say that the parable at times contains elements of other forms such as allegory, metaphor, and simile.

The parable was at the same time a method of revealing truth to the spiritually discerning and a method for concealing it from others whose hearts were not properly focused. Perhaps that is why Jesus used parables so often.

sower represents not just Jesus but anyone who lives as his representative on the earth. The sower is therefore any Christian in any generation who sows the word of God.

As a sower has the seed, so the messenger also has a message. The message of evangelism, the word of God, is the second element of evangelism. We are not merely to be witnesses about our pastor, our church, or our experience. We are to witness, first of all, about the word of God as it was manifest in Jesus Christ.

The third element in the process of evangelism is, of course, the soil, those who receive the message. Jesus' parable focused on this third element, identifying four kinds of responses to the word of God.

First, Jesus pictured the *unresponsive heart*, the person in whose life the word does not take root. Some people simply will not respond to God's word. Perhaps they have ill will toward the messenger. Or maybe they see the word of God as a threat because it strikes at the heart of their vested interests. Or maybe they are simply indifferent to the message, and before the word can take root in their lives, Satan has taken it away. When the word of God is sown, some ignore it. These have unresponsive hearts.

We are to witness, first of all, about the word of God as it was manifest in Jesus Christ.

Second, Jesus pictured the *impulsive heart*, those who instantaneously respond to the message with enthusiasm. Excitedly they declare, *This is for me*. But then, "when trouble or persecution comes because of the word, they quickly fall away" (4:17). "Trouble" refers to pressure from the outside. "Persecution" refers to actual suffering caused by outsiders. These fair-weather disciples think they want to follow Jesus, but when the pressure increases and the pain begins, they check out.

We see this response to the gospel today. Individuals hear the word of God and are attracted to it. It seems to meet their needs. It satisfies their deepest longings. As a result, they attend church. They may even try to articulate what God means to them. Yet, everything is merely on the surface. The word of God has not taken root in their heart. Consequently, when the hard times come and suffering strikes and pressures hit them, they say, *This is not what I thought it was.* And they silently slip away from the church.

The accumulation of wealth does not cause a person to say, Now, I have enough.

Jesus' clear statement about the perseverance of the saints in John 10:27–28—"'My sheep listen to my voice; I know them, and they follow me. I give them eternal life, and they shall never perish; no one can snatch them out of my hand'"—prevents us from interpreting this passage in Mark in such a way that suggests Christians fall from grace. More likely, Jesus had in mind those who presented the appearance of being believers but who never really became believers. His comment that "they have no root" (4:17) implies that they are not really believers. They are impulsive hearts that never really become transformed hearts.

Jesus identified a third response to the word of God: *preoccupied hearts* (4:18–19). Here we see not the indifference of the first response or the impulsive shallowness of the second response but a response that seems to be genuine. The seed does take root. The plant does spring up. And yet the fruit does not come because the plant is choked out by weeds that drain away the nourishment from the plant.

Jesus cited three factors that detract the believer from producing spiritual fruit. He mentioned "the worries of this life" (4:19). The root word for "worries" means to be drawn in different directions or to be pulled apart. A person can become so distracted by the world that he or she can be drawn away from the word of God.

Evangelizing the Reluctant

When I walked into the living room to visit the couple who had attended worship in our church, the wife told me, "You'll never make a Baptist out of me." Her husband joined the church alone, but she attended worship with him.

Several months later, she came by to see me. "I'm ready to publicly declare my faith in Christ," she told me, "but I'm not ready to be baptized yet." Her growth in Christ continued, culminating in her baptism about one year after our living room encounter. What can we do to create a climate for acceptance in those who are reluctant to take their stand?

Jesus also mentioned "the deceitfulness of wealth" (4:19). How is wealth deceitful? Increasing accumulation does not bring greater satisfaction. Instead, it generates greater hunger. The accumulation of wealth does not cause a person to say, *Now, I have enough.* Instead, accumulating wealth sends us to bed each night with the thought, *Tomorrow I must have more.* A person can get so caught up in the rat race of wanting more that the positive effect of the word of God can be neutralized.

These fair-weather disciples think they want to follow Jesus, but when the pressure increases and the pain begins, they check out.

Next Jesus mentioned "the desires for other things." A desire is a craving for something. "Other things" does not mean things that are bad but simply things that are non-essential. Christians can get so caught up in the affairs of this world that they have no time left for God. Thus the positive effect of the word of God is neutralized. Jesus' point is not that the word has not taken root but that it has not produced fruit. These individuals are preoccupied hearts who turn away from the opportunity to be productive hearts.

As the word of God is sown, Jesus promised, some will respond positively. These are *receptive hearts* in whose life the word of God takes root, for whom the word of God is top priority, through whom the fruit of the kingdom of God is produced. What a contrast with the unresponsive hearts and the shallow hearts and the preoccupied hearts. These receptive hearts hear the word of God because they want to hear it. They reflect on what they hear so they can reach a point of understanding. Then, they put the message into practice in their lives and bear fruit for the kingdom of God.

Implications for Us

We are reminded by Jesus' story of our responsibility to be evangelists. Some have been given the gift of evangelism according to the New Testament (Ephesians 4:11). However, all of us are to be evangelists, sharing the word of God with people we know. "How, then, can they call on the one they have not believed in? And how can they believe in the one of whom they have not heard? And how can they hear without someone preaching to them?" (Romans 10:14). This question should stir us every day as we wake up and each night as we go to bed. How will others hear the word of the gospel unless we tell them?

This was a parable of encouragement to the disciples, for the climax of the parable was the fertile soil that produced much fruit.

Jesus also reflected the varied responses that will be given to the message of the gospel. Not everyone will respond positively to the message of God. Some will be indifferent to it. Others will appear to accept it but will refuse to allow the message to touch their lives. Some will receive the word but, by their failure to rearrange their priorities, miss out on the fullness of the Christian life. And some will receive the word and produce abundant fruit for the kingdom of God. The response is determined, in each case, by the condition of the soil.

A person can become so distracted by the world that he or she can be drawn away from the word of God.

Further, Jesus affirmed the certainty of the results. This was a parable of encouragement to the disciples, for the climax of the parable was the fertile soil that produced much fruit. And it is a word of encouragement to disciples of every age. Often our work for Christ seems to be so ineffective. Our efforts seem to produce such infinitesimal result. Our labor seems to be wasted. However, this parable assures us a splendid harvest will come at the end of the day.

QUESTIONS

1. Why did Jesus teach in parables?
2. What does the parable of the sower tell us about the results of evangelism?
3. How can we sow the Word of God in the world today where much of the soil is either hardened or shallow?
4. How can we mobilize church members today to be sowers of the Word?

UNIT TWO

Showing His Power

An arsenal of powerful things greets us each day we live. Pervading our everyday life are such things as political power, peer power, intellectual power, electrical power, wealth power, and voting power, along with the power of sin, appetite, addiction, personality, and selfishness, to name only a few. Our faith affirms the reality of spiritual power and supernatural power. God intervenes in our world with the miraculous and is present through the Holy Spirit in his grace, love, mercy, and conviction of sin.

Mark's Gospel begins in chapter one by telling of the powerful things that Jesus was doing. Mark 1:27–28 relates, "The people were all so amazed that they asked each other, 'What is this? A new teaching—and with authority! He even gives orders to evil spirits and they obey him.' News about him spread quickly over the whole region of Galilee."

Unit Two, Showing His Power, focuses on Jesus' actions as recorded in Mark 4:35—8:38. These actions of Jesus further demonstrated his identity. They culminated in Mark 8:27–38 with the call for personal decision about who Jesus is. The emphasis in the first half of Mark's Gospel is on Jesus' power. This emphasis clarifies Jesus' identity and also sets the context for Jesus' beginning to teach about his suffering in Mark 8:31.

This series of lessons presents the supernatural power of Christ as proof of his identity and purpose as the genuine Son of God, the Anointed One, who came to rule with spiritual power and love.

UNIT TWO, SHOWING HIS POWER

Lesson 5	Jesus Demonstrates His Power	Mark 4:35–41; 5:21–43
Lesson 6	Jesus Shows Compassion for People	Mark 6:30–52
Lesson 7	Jesus Broadens His Ministry	Mark 7:1–8, 14–30
Lesson 8	Jesus Calls for Personal Decision	Mark 8:27–38

Focal Text

Mark 4:35–41;
5:21–43

Background

Mark 4:35–5:43

Main Idea

Jesus' victory over the storm and over disease and death confirm that he can help us in any difficulties we experience.

Question to Explore

What difference can Jesus actually make in the difficulties of our lives?

LESSON FIVE

Jesus Demonstrates His Power

Study Aim

To identify how I have experienced Jesus' loving care in the difficulties of my life

Study Actions and Emphases

- Share the gospel of Jesus Christ with all people
- Minister to human needs in the name of Jesus Christ
- Develop Christian families

Quick Read

Does Jesus care about people? The power of Christ over nature, disease, and death brings confidence that Jesus loves us and has the power to help in any difficulty we might experience.

Can Jesus make a difference in situations like these? A faithful Christian woman, recovering from an accident in which her foot was crushed, watched her husband, age fifty-seven, die suddenly before her very eyes. She asked, "Why would God want to take him when he wants to do so much for God and others?"

A friend attended her daughter in a Dallas hospital where the daughter was suffering excruciating pain from the most aggressive brain tumor. Her daughter was barely thirty-nine years old. She was a music leader in her church and a dynamic Christian witness.

My secretary just learned that her eye was deteriorating from diabetes, with doctors declaring her legally blind in one eye. A few days before, her stepfather had died and she was left to place her ill mother in a nursing home.

A young couple, parents for the first time, gave birth to a daughter born mentally and physically challenged. She died nine months later. Why did God not perform a miracle?

Physical futility, mental frustration, and spiritual apathy are often faced in such real life situations. At the same time, one can feel empowered in situations of such powerlessness. Empowerment can come through belief in the power of God. Through faith in Christ, losses are turned into gains.

Mark 4:35–41

35 That day when evening came, he said to his disciples,
"Let us go over to the other side." 36 Leaving the crowd
behind, they took him along, just as he was, in the boat.
There were also other boats with him. 37 A furious squall
came up, and the waves broke over the boat, so that it
was nearly swamped. 38 Jesus was in the stern, sleeping on
a cushion. The disciples woke him and said to him,
"Teacher, don't you care if we drown?"

39 He got up, rebuked the wind and said to the waves,
"Quiet! Be still!" Then the wind died down and it was
completely calm.

40 He said to his disciples, "Why are you so afraid? Do
you still have no faith?"

41 They were terrified and asked each other, "Who is
this? Even the wind and the waves obey him!"

Mark 5:21–43

21 When Jesus had again crossed over by boat to the
other side of the lake, a large crowd gathered around him
while he was by the lake. 22 Then one of the synagogue
rulers, named Jairus, came there. Seeing Jesus, he fell at his
feet 23 and pleaded earnestly with him, "My little daughter
is dying. Please come and put your hands on her so that
she will be healed and live." 24 So Jesus went with him.

A large crowd followed and pressed around him. 25 And
a woman was there who had been subject to bleeding

for twelve years. 26She had suffered a great deal under
the care of many doctors and had spent all she had, yet
instead of getting better she grew worse. 27When she
heard about Jesus, she came up behind him in the crowd
and touched his cloak, 28because she thought, "If I just
touch his clothes, I will be healed." 29Immediately her
bleeding stopped and she felt in her body that she was
freed from her suffering.

30At once Jesus realized that power had gone out from
him. He turned around in the crowd and asked, "Who
touched my clothes?"

31"You see the people crowding against you," his disci-
ples answered, "and yet you can ask, 'Who touched me?'"

32But Jesus kept looking around to see who had done it.
33Then the woman, knowing what had happened to her,
came and fell at his feet and, trembling with fear, told him
the whole truth. 34He said to her, "Daughter, your faith has
healed you. Go in peace and be freed from your suffering."

35While Jesus was still speaking, some men came from
the house of Jairus, the synagogue ruler. "Your daughter
is dead," they said. "Why bother the teacher any more?"

36Ignoring what they said, Jesus told the synagogue
ruler, "Don't be afraid; just believe."

37He did not let anyone follow him except Peter, James
and John the brother of James. 38When they came to the
home of the synagogue ruler, Jesus saw a commotion,
with people crying and wailing loudly. 39He went in and
said to them, "Why all this commotion and wailing? The
child is not dead but asleep." 40But they laughed at him.

After he put them all out, he took the child's father and mother and the disciples who were with him, and went
in where the child was. 41He took her by the hand and
said to her, *"Talitha koum!"* (which means, "Little girl, I
say to you, get up!"). 42Immediately the girl stood up and
walked around (she was twelve years old). At this they
were completely astonished. 43He gave strict orders not
to let anyone know about this, and told them to give her something to eat.

Power over Nature (4:35–41)

At the request of Jesus (4:35), the disciples, who were experienced boatmen, took Jesus "just as he was" (4:36), into a fishing vessel on a spontaneous journey to the other side of the lake. It was late in the afternoon, and Jesus was weary from a grueling day of teaching. It would be good to rest from the crowd and enjoy a relaxing boat ride at sunset. Sleeping during the violent storm would support the idea of Jesus' needing rest. The crowd could have followed by skirting the edge of the lake but did not because of the impending darkness and their own weariness. Mark tells us that other boats went along with them (4:37).

"A furious squall came up, and the waves broke over the boat" (4:37). The storm fell upon the lake, quickly making the waters wave with intensity and danger. Such experiences were common on this lake because of its location 682 feet below sea level and surrounded by mountains with open ravines that serve as wind tunnels. The heat from below draws down the cool air from above to create a clashing of atmospheres in a narrow space that causes a storm on the surface of the water. This was no ordinary storm but one in which the winds came with such outrage that the surface of the water was beaten into turbulent torrents. Mark wants us to know that the waves "broke over the boat" to dramatically describe the conditions endured that challenged them all (4:37). The tense of "broke over" shows repeated action of crashing into the boat over and over again.

Use your imagination to see the disciples rowing desperately and bailing water while holding on to keep from being washed overboard. There was no relief or respite from the power of the storm for their aching muscles and raging fear. The situation grew more and more desperate. Their strength was insufficient against such forces of nature.

"Why would God want to take him when he wants to do so much for God and others?"

Jesus "was in the stern" (4:38) of the boat. He was sleeping through the violent tossing of the boat, the pounding of the waves, the screaming of the wind, the thrashing of the oars, and the shouting by the disciples. The stern is the rear of the boat. It is the heaviest, most comfortable, most stable place on the boat. It is also where the steering takes place. Jesus lay on the rear seat with a cushion (4:38) under his head, with or

"Don't You Care?"

We can feel the intensity of the question in Mark 4:38 in the phrase, "Don't you care . . . ?" Christians often assume that when life brings storms, God is asleep and does not care. As this experience teaches, Jesus does care and has power to save and overcome the turbulence. Sometimes Jesus' help comes before our awareness, but often it comes after we ask. I am thoroughly convinced that Christ uses his many powers to bring calm to the storms in our lives. What personal situations have you experienced in which God empowered you and cared for you through particularly difficult times?

---

near the person steering the boat, perhaps Peter, James, or John, who steered the vessel toward its destination. It takes all of my imagination to visualize a sleeping Jesus in a fishing boat in a storm of this magnitude and intensity. This supports the idea of Jesus' human exhaustion and his total sense of assurance as the Son of God.

The force of the storm overwhelmed the disciples. They woke Jesus, saying to him (4:38), "Teacher, don't you care if we drown?" No feeling could be more natural than this. Their words, however, raise questions that clamor for insight. How should we interpret this in light of the overall experience? What should we suppose this should mean for us today? Their action was certainly expected, but their motivation is less clear. Did they wake Jesus as an act of compassion on their part to prepare to abandon ship, to rebuke him for not helping with the oars, or to seek to be saved through his power?

Jesus "got up, rebuked the wind and said to the waves, 'Quiet! Be still!'" (4:39) The present imperative tense means to *keep on being calm*. Immediately the wind died down, "and it was completely calm" (4:39).

Through faith in Christ, losses are turned into gains.

With nature's storm whimpering in peace, Jesus now turned to the harder task of encouraging faith. Though the disciples had agreed to follow him and had seen his mastery over disease and demons, they had not yet recognized him as the Son of God. Their understanding of Christ was far from complete. The question, "Do you still have no faith?" (4:40), tells us that their faith in Jesus hardly existed at all. Jesus had to work harder to encourage faith through the storm than to still the storm on the lake.

Fear is a powerful and self-centered emotion. Two different Greek words are used for fear. The word translated "afraid" (4:40) has the force of being cowardly. The word translated "terrified" (4:41) has the meaning of *awe* and *reverence*. The emotional fear of danger changed to a sacred awe and respect. Whatever fear the disciples had during the storm was even greater in the calm. They came to respect the Savior more than to fear the storm. Having seen this astounding power over nature, they turned their fear of nature to a fear of the One with power over nature.

We, too, are to fear more the One who is the Creator of our universe than we fear the troubles the natural universe brings. We see something of the mind of the disciples as they exclaimed (4:41), "'Who is this? Even the wind and the waves obey him!'"

Power over Disease and Death (5:21–34)

Crossing the lake back to Galilee, Jesus found another crowd and other crises. Jairus, a ruler of the synagogue, perhaps at Capernaum, organized worship and administered the services of the Jewish faith. It took courage for Jairus to come to Jesus. Jairus' position in the synagogue could be compromised if he came to Jesus.

Jesus had preached, taught, and healed in the synagogues, arousing the angry accusations of the scholars and teachers. Jairus probably had seen Jesus heal and heard him teach. The illness of Jairus' daughter made him more an agonized father than a leader of the synagogue, however. He ignored the forces of opposition and came with a powerful and desperate desire that his twelve-year-old daughter be healed. Jesus responded at once to go to the home of Jairus even as the crowds engulfed him, like a river of bodies pressing in on all sides.

They came to respect the Savior more than to fear the storm.

In the crowd was a woman with an incurable disease that caused bleeding that had plagued her for twelve years. Because of her bleeding she was considered unclean and treated like a leper. With strong faith, she touched Jesus on the hem of his garment. Immediately the bleeding stopped. Jesus felt the power go out of him. Jesus said to her, "' . . . Your faith has healed you. Go in peace and be freed of your suffering" (5:34). The woman knew by her own body that the bleeding had immediately stopped. When Jesus identified her with his eyes, she fell at his feet where she explained the whole truth about her faith and actions. She wanted simple healing and found a spiritual Savior. When we have a lifechanging encounter with the Lord Christ, we touch him on purpose, come in submission, and acknowledge the truth with honesty. After Jesus had dealt with this seeming interruption, he focused again on the daughter of Jairus.

Having seen this astounding power over nature, they turned their fear of nature to a fear of the One with power over nature.

Grief (5:35–41)

Some came from the house of Jairus to announce that his daughter was dead and Jesus was no longer needed. This was a critical moment. Death is finality, the hooded terror, the grim reaper. Jairus saw his hopes and dreams for his family come to an abrupt close. Jesus' response was astounding. He ignored their announcement and gave a simple answer, "'Don't be afraid; just believe'" (5:36). Faith always counters fear. Should Jairus give up, or trust Jesus? The answer would be the same even if the daughter had not been brought back to life. "Only believe" is the crucial response.

Peter, James, and John were invited to go with Jesus to witness the miracle. They arrived at the house to find chaotic grieving. "Wailing" is the translation of the word *alalazo* which incorporates the use of the

Teacher

"Teacher" (*didaskalos*), or instructor, is used often to refer to Jesus (Mark 4:38). "Teacher" denotes one who has teaching skills and thus can develop attitudes, apply wisdom, share great truths, and give excellence to performance. The disciples paid attention to Jesus, learned from his lessons, provided food, rowed and sailed the boat, helped manage the crowds, ran the errands, took some responsibility for Jesus' safety, joined him for the teaching sessions, and had the privilege of special insight through Jesus' explanations. However, Jesus was more than the truth he taught. Jesus asserted himself as the authoritative teacher who taught holy truth and, indeed, was himself that truth and the fulfillment of that truth. Christianity is more than a body of doctrine to learn and teach but is a personal relationship with the Christ who taught them.

sound (*alala*) of the word itself. Wailing was tumultuous and chaotic. Jesus interrupted the tumult with another astonishing statement, "'Why all this commotion and wailing? The child is not dead but asleep'" (5:39).

This statement by Mark lends the impression that the girl only seemed to be dead, perhaps in some kind of coma. The Greek word for "asleep" in 5:39 (*katheudei)* is a form of the word Mark used when referring to Jesus sleeping soundly in the stern of the boat (4:38). A different word (*koimao)* for sleep is used in John 11:11, when Lazarus was raised out of the grave, and in 1 Corinthians 15:6, 51 and 1 Thessalonians 4:13–14, when Paul obviously used "sleep" to refer to death. Matthew clearly has Jairus say, "'My daughter has just died'" (Matthew 9:18). Both of these Greek words, however, were used figuratively to mean death. The evidence is that Jesus meant the sleep of death.

The power of Christ will have the last word and final say in the drama of life and eternity.

Objections to the girl being in a coma include these: (1) Jesus specifically brought Peter, James, and John to the scene to witness this event of healing. (2) Family and friends were convinced she was dead and had already begun the grief process. (3) The crowd mocked Jesus for even suggesting she was only asleep. (4) Why would Jesus go to the trouble of clearing the room before approaching the girl if he were to only wake her from a coma? (5) Why would Jesus demand secrecy unless something extraordinary happened? "Asleep" is a metaphor of death and attests that the girl was dead but would not be for long.

Laughter

"But they laughed at him" (5:40). Those who laughed knew the child was dead. Laughing at Jesus in ridicule, they laughed and kept on laughing. The somberness of the circumstances was twisted into howling and snickering ridicule. The people's disbelief would eventually make a mockery of their own taunts. They might believe that the girl's body could be healed but never could death be reversed. The secular mind will often laugh at the resurrection and make fun of those who believe. The power of Christ will have the last word and final say in the drama of life and eternity.

Amazement

Jesus insisted everyone leave except for the parents and Peter, James, and John. Approaching the dead girl, he took her hand and spoke to her, saying, "'Little girl, I say to you, get up!'" (5:41) Mark records the instruction in Aramaic rather than Greek. Jesus knew that the power and authority of his voice would penetrate death itself and wake up the soul of anyone.

"Immediately" the girl got up and walked around. Immediately they who had previously laughed "were completely astonished" (5:42). Jesus had done the most remarkable miracle of all, bringing life out of death.

The resurrection of this girl was no doubt a foretaste of the resurrection of Christ himself. Jesus, the divine Son of God, has the power to raise the dead to life again. He provides experiential knowledge and stimulating motivation to believe in his own resurrection. Paul ties our resurrection to that of Jesus, "And if Christ has not been raised, our preaching is useless and so is your faith" (1 Corinthians 15:14). John, from his vision of the resurrected Lord, quotes Jesus, "I am the Living One; I was dead, and behold I am alive for ever and ever! And I hold the keys of death and Hades" (Revelation 1:18).

Jesus, the divine Son of God, has the power to raise the dead to life again.

QUESTIONS

1. In what situation have you felt powerless in your own strength but at the same time spiritually empowered?

2. What truths do we discover in these Scriptures that help us find calm while going through life's storms? How could Jesus sleep through such a storm?

3. How does Jesus address the issue of supernatural power in the created universe? How should we address supernatural power in our experience?

4. How does Jesus' power over all types of creation affect your view of him?

5. What part does the miraculous play in your life?

6. How does the experience of Jairus help us affirm the resurrection?

Focal Text

Mark 6:30–52

Background

Mark 6:1–52

Main Idea

Jesus shows compassion
for people who are experiencing
all sorts of troubles.

Question to Explore

How shall we treat people in need?

LESSON SIX Jesus Shows Compassion for People

Study Aim

To compare the way I treat people in need to the way Jesus did

Study and Action Emphases

- Share the gospel of Jesus Christ with all people
- Minister to human needs in the name of Jesus Christ
- Equip people for ministry in the church and in the world

Quick Read

Like Jesus, Christians should welcome opportunities to extend their compassion and be ready to help others in whatever way they can.

I stepped out of my office at the church and headed for the fellowship hall, not expecting what I discovered. I looked up to see a Hispanic man by the water fountain, face bruised and red. He was stifling tears of hurt and disappointment. I expressed astonishment and concern and asked what had happened. He explained in broken English through his sobs that he had been beaten. One of the men with whom he worked had sent him across the street to retrieve a truck. The co-worker knowingly had sent him into a fiasco. When he got into the truck, the owner came storming around the corner, thinking he was a thief. He pulled the man from the truck, threw him to the ground, and punched him out. As the man ran to escape, he saw his companions across the street bent over in laughter and mockery. The Hispanic man was agonizing in pain and panic. He was afraid that someone would follow him, and so he took refuge in the church. I assured him that he was safe. In frustration, he spoke to say, "I only want an opportunity, a small place where I can be accepted." He sought very little and hoped to find compassion and respect in a new environment.

Every person deserves compassion. Compassion is the heart and soul of our Christian faith. Jesus could not be the Christ without compassion. I was grateful that the man had sought compassion in the church and that I had an opportunity to counter violence with love. The lost world looks to the church for compassion and rightly so.

Mark 6:30–52

30 The apostles gathered around Jesus and reported to
him all they had done and taught. 31 Then, because so
many people were coming and going that they did not
even have a chance to eat, he said to them, "Come with
me by yourselves to a quiet place and get some rest."
32 So they went away by themselves in a boat to a soli-
tary place. 33 But many who saw them leaving recognized
them and ran on foot from all the towns and got there
ahead of them. 34 When Jesus landed and saw a large
crowd, he had compassion on them, because they were
like sheep without a shepherd. So he began teaching
them many things.
35 By this time it was late in the day, so his disciples
came to him. "This is a remote place," they said, "and
it's already very late. 36 Send the people away so they can
go to the surrounding countryside and villages and buy
themselves something to eat."
37 But he answered, "You give them something to eat."
They said to him, "That would take eight months of a
man's wages! Are we to go and spend that much on
bread and give it to them to eat?"
38 "How many loaves do you have?" he asked. "Go and
see."
When they found out, they said, "Five—and two fish."
39 Then Jesus directed them to have all the people sit
down in groups on the green grass. 40 So they sat down in
groups of hundreds and fifties. 41 Taking the five loaves

and the two fish and looking up to heaven, he gave thanks and broke the loaves. Then he gave them to his disciples to set before the people. He also divided the two fish among them all. [42]They all ate and were satisfied, [43]and the disciples picked up twelve basketfuls of broken pieces of bread and fish. [44]The number of the men who had eaten was five thousand.

[45]Immediately Jesus made his disciples get into the boat and go on ahead of him to Bethsaida, while he dismissed the crowd. [46]After leaving them, he went up on a mountainside to pray.

[47]When evening came, the boat was in the middle of the lake, and he was alone on land. [48]He saw the disciples straining at the oars, because the wind was against them. About the fourth watch of the night he went out to them, walking on the lake. He was about to pass by them, [49]but when they saw him walking on the lake, they thought he was a ghost. They cried out, [50]because they all saw him and were terrified.

Immediately he spoke to them and said, "Take courage! It is I. Don't be afraid." [51]Then he climbed into the boat with them, and the wind died down. They were completely amazed, [52]for they had not understood about the loaves; their hearts were hardened.

Understanding the Contrast Within the Context (6:1–34)

Following the healing of Jairus' daughter, Jesus left the shores of Galilee and went to his hometown, Nazareth.

The townspeople were stunned by his mighty works and his wisdom. Even more, they were offended. To them he could be only a simple carpenter, Mary's son, and "the brother of James, Joseph, Judas, and Simon" (6:3). Jesus found little compassion, only rejection and rebuke.

In frustration, he spoke to say, "I only want an opportunity, a small place where I can be accepted."

Preparing his disciples in knowledge and spirit, Jesus empowered them with authority over evil, instructed them as to their conduct, and then sent them out two by two into the villages of Galilee to benefit others. They did not have all the answers, and they did not understand completely the person of Christ (6:52). These novice disciples, commissioned by Jesus, put into practice what they had learned as they ministered to people, guided by the objectives of their Teacher.

King Herod had placed John the Baptist in prison because John had rebuked Herod for his adulterous, incestuous, unlawful marriage to Herodius, the wife of his brother, Philip. Herod feared John and protected him, impressed that he was a righteous man. Herodius, carrying a grudge over the rebuke, wanted revenge. Herodius' daughter danced to entertain Herod and his guests at his wild birthday party. She so pleased Herod that he offered her anything she wanted up to half of his kingdom. Conferring with her spiteful mother, she asked for the head of John the Baptist. John's head was soon brought to her on a platter.

Hardly would one find an experience of less compassion. Herod, Herodius, and the daughter were all caught up in their hateful lives of selfishness, indulgence, debauchery, pleasure, and inhumanity. As Christ acted with compassion, the leaders of that culture practiced their hateful thoughts of vengeance and violence. Although Herod had heard the message of repentance, his own head and heart would not turn from sin. The kingly court became exemplary of what Christianity faces in today's secular world. An unrepentant heart results in a world empty and void of godly compassion for others.

Every person deserves compassion.

A Ministry of Rest and Retreat (6:30–34)

Returning from their strenuous mission of preaching and healing, the disciples were weary and worn. Yet, imagine their excitement as they shared with Jesus the stories of their experiences. What they had seen Jesus say and do, they had done.

Jesus had compassion on the disciples and led them into retreat for rest from the stress of their own ministry, a violent Herod, the fanaticism of the crowds, and the hostility of the Jewish leaders. He took the initiative and led them by boat to the northeastern shores of Galilee, an area that was isolated and deserted, a place of privacy and sanctuary, saying, "'Come with me by yourselves to a quiet place and get

Compassion

The Greek word translated "compassion" in Mark 6:34 and 8:2 is a form of the word *splanchnizomai,* which is a verb. The verb came to denote the emotional inner disposition that leads to mercy and pity. It is a forceful term to express the deepest level of the whole personality in showing mercy, sympathy, and concern. Philippians 1:8 suggests that this kind of compassion is possible only through our relationship with Christ.

---

some rest'" (6:31). Jesus knew that if the disciples were to be enablers, they must be enabled; if they would be healers, they must seek healing themselves; if they would lead spiritually, they must have spiritual food; if they were to give gifts to others, they must receive gifts from God.

I asked recently about a minister friend who had resigned his church. The church member with whom I spoke shared that he was young and inexperienced and could not meet the challenges of a large pastorate. He had burned out, succumbed to the stress, neglected his own needs, and left the ministry. Life can become so busy that spiritual growth is improbable or impossible. Meeting human need can be the most stressful of all joys. As rewarding as it can be, it also drains strength through exhaustion. Many individuals have fallen into sin because of the strain and drain of long hours of work without seeking rest and retreat. Depleting physical resources also depletes emotional and spiritual resources. Such becomes the environment of moral and leadership failures. Our Lord teaches us that there are times when one must have compassion for self.

Compassion is the heart and soul of our Christian faith.

Rest is not always possible when needed. When one stands on the northwestern shore of the Sea of Galilee, the opposite shore is visible. The crowd anticipated the direction of the boat and quickly ran around the shoreline. They were waiting when Jesus arrived. Though more weary now, he "had compassion on them, because they were like sheep without a shepherd" (6:34).

A Ministry of Resources (Mark 6:35–44)

In late afternoon, after 3:00 PM, the people were tired, hungry, and restless. They had not eaten since morning. The frenzied excitement of following Jesus around the lake allowed no time to prepare appropriately. Notice that the disciples alerted Jesus to the condition of the people and suggested that he send them away from this remote spot so they could "'buy themselves something to eat'" (6:36). This was a huge crowd of 5000 men plus women and children (6:44).

Sending them away was the only reasonable solution the disciples knew. The problem was too big for small thinking. Jesus' response, "'You give them something to eat'" (6:37), suggests that the disciples did have some resources. The two verbs, "send" (6:36) and "give" (6:37), are completely different reactions to the same human needs. "Send" acknowledges the impending need of hunger and nourishment with no available supply of food or the finances necessary to purchase it. "Give" acknowledges the same need and that the Father's sufficient resources were available.

Jesus subtracted by getting down to one solution of five loaves and two fish, added by looking to heaven and giving thanks, divided when he broke the loaves and fish, and multiplied with twelve baskets left over.

The disciples asked (6:37), "'Are we to go and spend that much on bread and give it to them to eat?'" Their question could imply that sufficient funding or food was available from some source, perhaps the pockets of the crowd or the disciples themselves. The NIV translation makes clear that feeding such a crowd would cost eight months of one person's earned wages (6:37). Whenever there is a need, there are always those who would push the responsibility on someone else and also those who would try to meet the need the best way they can. Jesus provides resources to help those who help and those who need help.

A mathematical miracle of ministry took place. Jesus subtracted by getting down to one solution of five loaves and two fish, added by looking to heaven and giving thanks, divided when he broke the loaves and fish, and multiplied with twelve baskets left over. Jesus organized the crowd in groups for efficiency. In the Greek of 6:41, the tenses of the verbs indicate that Jesus broke the bread and fish and then *kept on* giving the food to the disciples who *kept on* setting it before the people.

The disciples calculated within limited impossibilities while Christ calculated with unlimited possibilities. Christ teaches us that in any situation the abundant resources of God are always available to extend our meager resources. What was the conclusion of the miracle? "They all ate and were satisfied" (6:42).

Nothing is too big for our God. Leave any limitations to him. Keep open to the impossible. Liberate

---

Insights for Ministry

Insights for ministry can be drawn from the feeding of the 5000:

- Disciples of our Lord have responsibility for those in need.
- Followers of Christ should be willing to use what they have.
- If we do not have adequate resources, we should look around for what might be available.
- Once we give God what we have, God will multiply its use and effectiveness.

---

your vision to think outside the boundaries of the possible. With Jesus, a little is a lot.

It would be difficult for us today to conceive of Christ as the divine Son of God without the miraculous. Mark's Gospel underlines the miracles of Jesus. Understanding the natural mindset of individuals, Mark intends through the written narrative to give evidence of the credibility of Jesus as the Savior by telling of the miracles. Jesus lived in a critical and hostile atmosphere. It was necessary to objectify the supernatural power of Christ in this material world if Christ were to be recognized. The miraculous provided the visible proof to thousands of witnesses. Miraculous experiences dominate the sixteen chapters of Mark.

> *Christ teaches us that in any situation the abundant resources of God are always available to extend our meager resources.*

Miracles continue to be mysterious. Miracles are more than subjects for thought and study. They should never be beyond our faith. One can believe in supernatural miracles of the New Testament without seeing those same kinds of experiences today. One can believe in miracles without experiencing them personally. Miracles are always possible through prayer. God's authority, power, and will are superior at all times to any of God's natural laws in this universe. God still has power, and we still need faith.

Because of the presence of the written word as testimony to our Lord, miracles are not so necessary today. Often, so-called miracles are but false sensationalism by shysters to fleece money from the unsuspecting and entice well-meaning followers. People are by nature more interested in the physical than the spiritual. Christ, however, avoided the sensationalism (see 5:43) that often accompanies people known as healers today. Christ's purpose and greatest miracle is the saving of the soul. "For the Son of Man came to seek and save what was lost" (Luke 19:10).

Nothing is too big for our God.

A Ministry of Readiness (Mark 6:45–52)

Once the miracle was completed, Jesus immediately insisted the disciples go ahead of him to Bethsaida. He dismissed the crowds and went into the hills for prayer. We can only guess as to why Jesus was so insistent that the disciples leave. Perhaps they contributed to the commotion of the crowd, they had served their usefulness regarding the momentous event, they were being pressed to become political leaders, or they were exhausted from the long day and should continue to find a private place.

Why should anyone who knows Jesus be afraid?

As the disciples rowed away toward their destination, the winds blew against them. Jesus, alone on the shore at twilight, observed them "straining at the oars" (6:48). "About the fourth watch of the night" (6:48), which would have been between three and six in the morning, Jesus came walking on the lake. The disciples in the boat thought Jesus was an apparition, a ghost. They were terrified. They cried out or screamed out. Jesus identified himself and climbed into the boat, calming both their fear and the sea.

In Mark 4:35–41, the disciples had seen Jesus calm the storm on this same lake. They seem as much amazed the second time as the first. Mark notes that they "had not understood about the loaves; their hearts were hardened" (6:52). The disciples were slow learners rather than being opposed to Christ. What they were experiencing was so amazing and shocking that comprehension was beyond them. They could not absorb the new truths so quickly.

God still has power, and we still need faith.

If the disciples were struggling, one can imagine how the rest of the crowd was bewildered. Could they accept what they saw? Who was this man from Nazareth with such uncommon wisdom and supernatural power?

The disciples, like each of us, were so oriented to earth that seeing with the heart was like looking through a veil that obscured the view. Regardless of what they missed, the compassionate Christ was there with them to put all circumstances of anxiety and challenges to his authority under his feet.

Why should anyone who knows Jesus be afraid? Jesus is always vigilant in our distress, always present in our turbulence, always ready to make the impossible possible. Jesus may just pass us by (6:48) unless we see him and cry for his help. In the howl of the storm, "Take courage! It is I. Don't be afraid" (6:50).

QUESTIONS

1. How do you express compassion as a Christian virtue? to those outside your normal circle of family and friends? to those who are your enemies?

2. How do the two different responses, "Send the people away," and "Give them something to eat" (6:36–36), characterize your discipleship? your church? What are the evidences that the disciples had compassion on the crowds?

3. Does God still do miracles today? Share with the class your experience with a recent miracle. Share an experience in which a solution to help someone came unexpectedly.

4. How does Christ combine social ministry with the teaching of his word? How do your insights on this question impact your philosophy of missions? In doing the work of missions, should Christians build hospitals, orphanages, and other such institutions, and engage in agricultural missions?

5. What does your church do to help others? Does your church offer opportunities to get involved in helping ministries? Should you depend on the church to make you aware of needs?

6. How much money and time did you give in the past month to meet the needs of others outside your family?

Focal Text

Mark 7:1–8, 14–30

Background

Mark 6:53—8:10

Main Idea

Jesus breaks down the barriers of human traditions that people sometimes try to erect to restrict access to God's salvation.

Question to Explore

What barriers do we insist that people cross to have access to God's salvation?

LESSON SEVEN

Jesus Broadens His Ministry

Study Aim

To identify any human barriers that restrict access to God's salvation

Study and Action Emphases

- Share the gospel of Jesus Christ with all people
- Minister to human needs in the name of Jesus Christ
- Equip people for ministry in the church and in the world
- Develop Christian families
- Strengthen existing churches and start new congregations

Quick Read

Jesus never allowed barriers to restrict him. Obedience, courage, and determination can break through the barriers and strongholds that separate people and cultures.

Some years ago in Rio de Janeiro, following a meal, I found myself witnessing to an employee of the restaurant. I was an American Anglo sharing Christ with a man who was African by nationality, black by race, with Portuguese as his language and Brazilian as his culture, and who believed in witchcraft. The grace of God reached down to him as he prayed the prayer of salvation. For me, it was a unique opportunity that opened another window to my world. Many barriers of culture, race, nationality, and language came down as the gospel was presented.

Barriers can be erected from both directions of a relationship. These are the unholy three: tradition, hypocrisy, and prejudice. The barrier of tradition stifles the heart, the barrier of prejudice spurns the worth of another, and the barrier of hypocrisy belittles truth. Christianity constantly batters away at barriers, breaking them down to make the gospel more accessible.

The Barrier of Senseless Ceremony (7:1–5)

Opposition to Jesus was building. Jesus was often welcomed into the local synagogues of Galilee (Mark 1:29, 39; 3:1; 6:2), where he was invited to teach. In Mark 7:1, the Pharisees and scribes from Jerusalem were less accommodating and more hostile. They came to do their own investigation and to evaluate the doctrines and teaching of this religious rebel. Why did Jesus not practice and observe "the tradition

Mark 7:1–8, 14–30

1The Pharisees and some of the teachers of the law who
had come from Jerusalem gathered around Jesus and 2saw
some of his disciples eating food with hands that were
"unclean," that is, unwashed. 3(The Pharisees and all the
Jews do not eat unless they give their hands a ceremonial
washing, holding to the tradition of the elders. 4When
they come from the marketplace they do not eat unless
they wash. And they observe many other traditions, such
as the washing of cups, pitchers and kettles.)

5So the Pharisees and teachers of the law asked Jesus,
"Why don't your disciples live according to the tradition
of the elders instead of eating their food with 'unclean'
hands?"

6He replied, "Isaiah was right when he prophesied
about you hypocrites; as it is written:

"'These people honor me with their lips,
but their hearts are far from me.
7 They worship me in vain;
their teachings are but rules taught by men.'

8You have let go of the commands of God and are hold-
ing on to the traditions of men."

● ●

14Again Jesus called the crowd to him and said, "Listen
to me, everyone, and understand this. 15Nothing outside
a man can make him 'unclean' by going into him.

Rather, it is what comes out of a man that makes him
'unclean.'"
17After he had left the crowd and entered the house, his
disciples asked him about this parable. 18"Are you so dull?"
he asked. "Don't you see that nothing that enters a man
from the outside can make him 'unclean'? 19For it doesn't
go into his heart but into his stomach, and then out of his
body." (In saying this, Jesus declared all foods "clean.")
20He went on: "What comes out of a man is what
makes him 'unclean.' 21For from within, out of men's
hearts, come evil thoughts, sexual immorality, theft,
murder, adultery, 22greed, malice, deceit, lewdness, envy,
slander, arrogance and folly. 23All these evils come from
inside and make a man 'unclean.'"
24Jesus left that place and went to the vicinity of Tyre. He
entered a house and did not want anyone to know it; yet
he could not keep his presence secret. 25In fact, as soon as
she heard about him, a woman whose little daughter was
possessed by an evil spirit came and fell at his feet. 26The
woman was a Greek, born in Syrian Phoenicia. She
begged Jesus to drive the demon out of her daughter.
27"First let the children eat all they want," he told her,
"for it is not right to take the children's bread and toss it
to their dogs."
28"Yes, Lord," she replied, "but even the dogs under
the table eat the children's crumbs."
29Then he told her, "For such a reply, you may go; the
demon has left your daughter."
30She went home and found her child lying on the bed,
and the demon gone.

of the elders" (7:3)? The differences between Jesus' teaching and Jewish traditions were glaringly clear. Confrontation with Jesus brought to the surface the reason for his rejection of the legalistic traditions of his ancestors.

The law for the Jews meant the Pentateuch (the first five books of the Old Testament). The Jewish law also came to include an oral tradition called the "tradition of the elders" (7:3), constituting thousands of rules and regulations contrived as expansions and amplifications of the written law to govern any kind of situation in life. These rules or laws were applied in ways that were unjustified and ridiculous. Three centuries later, these unwritten laws were written down in a book called the Mishnah. This oral law included a specific rigid ceremony of washing hands and cleansing cups, pitchers, kettles, and other vessels (7:4).

These Jewish leaders observed the disciples eating food with hands that were ceremonially unclean (7:2). The word translated "unclean" is the word *koinais*, meaning *common*. "Unclean," as used here, has nothing to do with hygiene or manners but rather refers to that which is ceremonially profane rather than ceremonially sacred. The disciples' hands were considered profane and unfit in the sight of God. William Barclay notes on this passage that the view in that day was that ceremonially unwashed hands made one subject to attack by a demon.[1]

"Traditions" (7:4) has a negative sense, referring to additions to the law of God and practiced only because of ceremony. Jesus rejected the validity of such additions as teachings not having divine authority. The Pharisees and scribes considered legalistic observances of this nature as the essence of true religion. To break the traditions of ceremonial law was defilement and sin. The Pharisees considered these traditional external acts to constitute holiness and morality.

It may seem very difficult for Baptist minds to comprehend such folly and nonsense. However, we would do well to consider the place we allow our own traditions to have in our church culture.

The Barrier of Heartless Hypocrisy (7:6–8)

Jesus quoted Isaiah the prophet, whom the Pharisees read and revered, to answer their question of why the disciples ignored the tradition of ceremonial washing. Jesus spoke with boldness, "'Isaiah was right when he prophesied about you hypocrites'" (7:6). Jesus explained their hypocrisy, quoting from Isaiah 29:13. God accused Israel of honoring him "with their lips, but their hearts are far from me" (Mark 7:6).

The differences between Jesus' teaching and Jewish traditions were glaringly clear.

Thus Jesus discounted the authority of the Pharisees' traditions as "'rules taught by men'" (7:7), inappropriate and unauthorized contrived additions to

Hypocrisy

Hypocrisy, a word that is transliterated from the Greek word, means *to play the hypocrite.*

The word *hypocrisy* referred to an actor who interpreted a role or played a part on stage. The word took on the sense of pretense without sincerity.

Hypocrisy had a very negative connotation as concealment of truth with self-contradiction. In disguise, a person pretended to be good or put on a mask to hide the real self. The hypocrite was a false teacher who taught with deceitfulness. In the case of the Pharisees and scribes, their hypocrisy connected with ritual and tradition without a sense of correct attitudes and thoughts. Goodness was equated to the legalistic ritual itself rather than an obedient heart. The word refers in general to any kind of pretense or deception.

---

divine instruction. Human rules had replaced the divine instructions from God (7:8). The accusers had no response to Jesus' accusation.

How hypocritical were these Pharisees and scribes? Jesus continued to drop the hammer by exposing the defilement of their hearts. He had given them a general insight and now became specific in 7:9 in showing what he meant by their "setting aside the commands of God in order to observe your own traditions!" The example, one of many that could have been given (7:13), was how the tradition of "Corban" was used to nullify God's word to honor one's father and mother (7:11). When something was "Corban," it was considered sacred and could be used for no other purpose than the work of God. The traditions of the elders allowed a person to evade responsibility for care of one's parents by declaring one's resources "Corban," sacred unto God. Such diversion was but a clever deceit from the mind of Satan but unveiled by the knowing wisdom of Christ.

Verbally undressing the sins of the spiritual leaders, Jesus called the crowd in close to be sure that the people could hear, understand the main lesson, and see the hypocrisy of the Pharisees (7:14). The sin of hypocrisy is still with us in many different forms. Goodness is equated with being a decent citizen, husband, or father. Serving God with outward things such as church attendance, Bible study, deeds of service, giving money, teaching, and preaching can all become nothing more than rituals that mask hateful attitudes and secret disobedience. There are times in which everyone is a hypocrite. Hypocrisy can be subtle so that what once was done for the right reason becomes nothing more than a reasonable rite.

The Heart of the Matter (7:14–23)

Barclay declares these verses some of the most revolutionary in the New Testament.[2] Here Jesus destroyed and buried the rules for which the Jews had lived and died. Orthodox Jews to this day take seriously the list of unclean animals in Leviticus 11. During the abusive persecution by Antiochus Epiphanes, between the Old and New Testaments, many Jews chose death rather than eat the flesh of pigs. In the parable of the prodigal son (Luke 15:11–32), the greatest degradation of the son who went away was eating with the swine. Jesus' teaching in Mark 7:14–23 is a foretaste of Peter's vision on the rooftop with a voice telling him, "Kill and eat," with Peter responding, "I have never eaten anything impure or unclean" (Acts 10:13–14).

Serving God with outward things such as church attendance, Bible study, deeds of service, giving money, teaching, and preaching can all become nothing more than rituals that mask hateful attitudes and secret disobedience.

The crowd must have dropped their jaws in shock when Jesus said, "Nothing outside a man can make him 'unclean' by going into him" (Mark 7:15). Jesus had stuck his finger on another nerve of tradition.

Exceeding the best of lawyers, Jesus presented his case. He exposed ceremonial handwashing as irrelevant, charged that human traditions (for example, "Corban," 7:11) were used to disobey the very word of God, and declared that corruption and "evils come from inside, and make a man 'unclean'" (7:23). Jesus called the disciples "dull" (7:18), or undiscerning, when they did not comprehend his teaching. Their thoughts were on unclean food as external defilement while Jesus championed the internal source where sin is conceived and chosen within the mind and heart. Jesus explained it to them a second time (7:17–19), giving specific illustrations (7:20–23). Out of the heart, from within, come such things as "evil thoughts, sexual immorality, theft, murder, adultery, greed, malice, deceit, lewdness, envy, slander, arrogance and folly" (7:21–22). A genuine relationship to God is not based on accurate repetitions of rites but on repentance. Turning to God brings change to the inside, where pure hearts are cleansed before the Lord God.

A genuine relationship to God is not based on accurate repetitions of rites but on repentance.

Jesus' teaching on this matter was a new concept to his disciples. New concepts are hard to absorb. See this as a major turning point in the events leading toward a full understanding of Jesus' kingdom. Jesus came to save people from their sin and self rather than bless stale rites and unauthorized traditions. Jesus was aware of how hard it is to pour new wine into old wineskins (2:19–22).

When in college I attended a revival service in a nearby church to hear a pastor I admired. During the message he told a personal story that happened when he was in the military helping liberate the Nazi concentration camps of Europe. As he and his fellow soldiers approached one of the concentration camps, word had already spread that the soldiers were arriving. The gates were opened for the prisoners to come out to greet them. The prisoners hobbled out in horrible condition, bodies emaciated, diseased, and covered with filth. The prisoners' gratitude was so compelling that they offered the soldiers the only thing they had—bread. The bread came from grateful hearts but in filthy, grimy, diseased, unwashed hands. The liberating soldiers accepted their awesome gratitude but refused to accept the pure, clean bread from such filthy hands. The Pharisees offered God to their world with clean hands but unclean hearts. Jesus obviously prefers the former. It is the inside that counts.

Jesus came to save people from their sin and self rather than bless stale rites and unauthorized traditions.

The Barrier of Proud Prejudice (7:24–30)

Following the confrontation with the traditional, ritualistic, and hypocritical religion of the Pharisees, Jesus needed rest and quiet. He withdrew from Galilee to a location near Tyre, some forty miles to the northwest. He chose a place with the intention of anonymity, where he could recover from the stress upon his soul and body (7:24).

This experience with this Gentile woman could suggest a deliberate intention to open a window to the pagan world, a concept that would take time for the disciples to process. Whether this event was coincidental or intentional, Jesus continued to teach the

Ritual, Hypocrisy, Prejudice

These unholy three—ritual, hypocrisy, and prejudice—are examples of externalized religion at its worst. Fulfilling the outward form, many think that they are acceptable before God. These concepts offer a false Christianity and are powerful barriers to evangelism. Unsaved people see through these conditions easily. Worship has to be genuine, honest, truthful, sincere, real, and authentic. Consider how these three ideas impact worship in your church and in your life. How does Jesus see and receive us when we worship with these conditions in our lives? Can genuine worship take place under these conditions? What do you think?

disciples. Mark must have included the passage to show that Jesus was full of mercy and compassion for everyone and anyone.

The woman was the epitome of the mission field. She was Phoenician by race and was a descendant of the Canaanites, the original inhabitants of the land of Israel. She likely had a Greek religion and spoke Syrian. Everything about this Gentile woman was offensive to Jewish pride and prejudice. However, she was open to receiving the mercy of Christ. Christians will often avoid relationships and ministry because of the same prejudices and exclusiveness that are suggested here. Tyre represents any place on earth where people have needs. Jesus applied his power to people's needs, regardless of race, language, culture, color, or position.

Immediately upon hearing of Jesus' presence, the woman moved beyond the racial barriers. She went to Jesus and "fell at His feet" (7:25). "She begged Jesus to drive the demon out of her daughter" (7:26). Whatever else the woman was, she was a mother with a mother's heart in sorrow over her ill child. As Jairus ignored his place in the synagogue to seek healing for his daughter, this woman ignored the racial division to ask for Jesus' power. The agony she had for her child pushed aside any sense of prejudice between a Gentile and a Jew. She brought her request to Jesus.

Christians will often avoid relationships and ministry because of the same prejudices and exclusiveness that are suggested here.

The response of Jesus in Mark 7:27 seems strange and confusing to us but was apparently understood by this woman who was more familiar with the two different cultures. Perhaps the statement by Christ was only part of a larger discussion. Why would Jesus respond with such a statement that appears completely out of context? Was it a harsh rebuke for the woman's interruption? Was it some kind of test of her faith or some sort of veiled meaning?

Look beyond the words of Jesus' response to his sense of humor and tenderness. In the statement, "First let the children eat all they want . . . for it is not right to take the children's bread and toss it to their dogs" (7:27), Jesus used the diminutive meaning little dogs or puppies (*kunariois*) rather than the usual word for dog (*kunos*). With quickness of wit, she replied, "'Yes, Lord, but even the dogs [*kunaria*] under the table eat the children's crumbs" (7:28).

Consider the possibilities of this passage. Was the strategy of taking the gospel first to the children of Israel suddenly set aside because of the woman's insight and wit? Did the woman see the "puppy" word as a reference to her and other Gentiles and the bread a symbol of the gospel or the resources of Jesus? Was she thus begging for a crumb of Jesus' power for her daughter? Was Jesus expressing the typical attitude of the Jew but then setting it aside to teach the disciples a lesson? Perhaps Jesus sought to undercut the feelings of prejudice within the framework of the conversation to soften the hearts of the disciples toward this woman's need.

No national, racial, cultural, or language barrier would stand in the way of reaching out to all people in their world.

There are more questions than answers. However, the main lesson is clear. No national, racial, cultural, or language barrier would stand in the way of reaching out to all people in their world. Risking humiliation and recognizing Jesus as Lord, the woman exercised her faith until there was an answer. A most unlikely person received what she asked. "She went home and found her child lying on the bed, and the demon gone" (7:30).

QUESTIONS

1. When does tradition become senseless ceremony? Can traditions be good?

2. What are some of the traditions in your church that become barriers to the gospel?

3. What is an *unauthorized* tradition? Name some in your church.

4. Explain and enumerate examples of hypocrisy that you see in your church, in your own life. Is hypocrisy a major issue in reaching the lost? What do you do about it?

5. Explain the importance of faith in dealing with unauthorized traditions, hypocrisy, and prejudice.

6. The typical response to the gospel by an unsaved person is, "I am a good person." How is that hypocritical? How can you overcome that barrier?

NOTES

1. William Barclay, *The Gospel of Mark*, The Daily Study Bible (Philadelphia: The Westminster Press, 1956), 167.
2. Barclay, 174.

Focal Text

Mark 8:27–38

Background

Mark 8:11–38

Main Idea

Jesus calls people to commit themselves fully to him, regardless of the cost.

Question to Explore

Who do *you* say Jesus is?

LESSON EIGHT

Jesus Calls for Personal Decision

Study Aim

To commit myself to follow Jesus fully, regardless of the cost

Study and Action Emphases

- Share the gospel of Jesus Christ with all people
- Minister to human needs in the name of Jesus Christ
- Equip people for ministry in the church and in the world

Quick Read

Discovering the true identify of Jesus as the Son of God calls us to follow him regardless of whatever disgrace, rejection, sacrifice, inconvenience, or persecution may come.

A recent issue of *U. S. News and World Report*[1] carried an article on "China's Christian Underground." Christians in China brave the government's fury and vengeance by living out their faith and worship of Christ. All over China, small groups in house churches meet secretly for worship, training, and encouragement.

Legal churches exist in China but are controlled by the Communist government. Each Sunday these legal churches are filled to capacity with some fifteen million Protestants and five million Catholics. The number of underground Christians is unknown but is estimated to be at least five times more Protestants and twice as many Catholics as are in the legal churches.

These Christians willingly choose to risk their freedom, torture, and martyrdom. For them to worship in the legal churches means ultimate allegiance to the Communist party rather than God. Their strategy is not revolution but transformation of individuals who then change institutions of power. Suffering for Christ becomes beneficial as a test of their faith and love. They are aggressively evangelistic and have a passion to see their country come to Christ regardless of the cost.

The Background (7:31—8:26)

Following the healing of the daughter of the Gentile woman in Tyre, Jesus "went through Sidon, down to the Sea of Galilee and into the region of the Decapolis" (7:31). Mark tells us that Jesus healed a man of

Mark 8:27–38

27 Jesus and his disciples went on to the villages around
Caesarea Philippi. On the way he asked them, "Who do
people say I am?"
28 They replied, "Some say John the Baptist; others say
Elijah; and still others, one of the prophets."
29 "But what about you?" he asked. "Who do you say I
am?"
Peter answered, "You are the Christ."
30 Jesus warned them not to tell anyone about him.
31 He then began to teach them that the Son of Man must
suffer many things and be rejected by the elders, chief
priests and teachers of the law, and that he must be killed
and after three days rise again. 32 He spoke plainly about
this, and Peter took him aside and began to rebuke him.
33 But when Jesus turned and looked at his disciples, he
rebuked Peter. "Get behind me, Satan!" he said. "You do
not have in mind the things of God, but the things of men."
34 Then he called the crowd to him along with his disci-
ples and said: "If anyone would come after me, he must
deny himself and take up his cross and follow me. 35 For
whoever wants to save his life will lose it, but whoever
loses his life for me and for the gospel will save it. 36 What
good is it for a man to gain the whole world, yet forfeit
his soul? 37 Or what can a man give in exchange for his
soul? 38 If anyone is ashamed of me and my words in this
adulterous and sinful generation, the Son of Man will be
ashamed of him when he comes in his Father's glory
with the holy angels."

deafness (7:32–37). The geographical location indicates that the man was a Gentile. Thus Jesus again was teaching the disciples that the gospel was for anyone, Gentile or Jew. If there were any doubt, the feeding of the 4,000 (Mark 8:1–10) would drive home this truth further. They, too, likely were Gentiles as indicated by the fact that the word for "basketfuls" in 8:8 referred to the kind of basket used mainly by Gentiles. In contrast, the Greek word translated "basketfuls" in 6:43 referred to the basket used mainly by Jews.

Getting into a boat (8:10), Jesus crossed the lake again from east to west to Dalmanutha, probably in the vicinity of Tiberius. The Pharisees joined the crowd and asked for a sign from heaven. Jesus refused to give them one (8:11–13). Crossing the lake again from the west to the northeast, he came to Bethsaida, where he healed a blind man (8:22–26). On the way across, the disciples realized they had brought only one loaf of bread (8:14). Jesus' remarks to them may indicate both serious teaching and humor (8:15–21). How ironic that they were concerned about having no bread when Jesus had just fed 4,000 people. Jesus admonished them for their slowness to understand.

Revealing the Christ (8:27–30)

After months and many experiences of Jesus' teaching, miracles, and self-disclosure, the disciples faced a time of testing. Jesus wanted them to understand who he was, what they had learned about him, and where their journey was leading. Jesus asked two questions, one leading to the other, moving from the general to the specific. A crucial turning point in the ministry of Jesus was taking place.

These Christians willingly choose to risk their freedom, torture, and martyrdom.

These same crucial questions are asked of all people in every generation. When we are tested, we must make a decision, too. Choosing whether to follow Christ is essential for everyone.

Leaving Bethsaida and moving twenty-five miles to the northeast, Jesus led the disciples to the region of Caesarea Philippi, on the very northern edge of Israel, at the foot of Mt. Hermon where the transfiguration would soon take place (9:1–8). Caesarea meant *Caesar's town*, where Herod the Great had built a white marble temple to Caesar Augustus. The city was a center of emperor worship. Herod Philip, to distinguish the town from the Caesarea on the seacoast, added his name to it. In this environment with symbols of paganism and emperor worship found in abundance, Jesus asked the first question (8:27), "Who do people say I am?" This probing question came in a conspicuous setting at a strategic time.

Choosing whether to follow Christ is essential for everyone.

The disciples answered, "Some say John the Baptist; others say Elijah; and still others, one of the prophets"

(8:28; see 6:14–15). Some thought Jesus was Elijah because of Malachi 4:5–6. The point of view of the people had not changed from earlier, holding Jesus up with great regard and respect but identifying him with their saintly ancestors. Later, at the transfiguration, Elijah appeared with Moses, and they spoke with Jesus (Mark 9:4–5). The Father said, "This is my Son, whom I love. Listen to him" (9:7). The transfiguration provided a clear identification of the person of Christ. When Elijah and Moses disappeared, the disciples saw no one "except Jesus" (9:8).

Jesus was telling Peter that he had missed the point and still had much to learn before he grasped the deeper meaning of who Jesus was and what Jesus was doing.

Jesus then asked the second, more specific question (8:29), "But what about you? . . . Who do you say I am?" The construction of the Greek sentences gives a triple emphasis on the word "you." The word is written in, placed at the first of the sentence, and included in the verb. Peter answered, "You are the Christ" (8:29). "Christ" is from the Greek word, and "Messiah" indicates the Hebrew title for the Anointed One of God, the one of old who would rule over the nations of this earth. As the Christ, Jesus would be the King, Priest, Prophet, and Deliverer.

The disciples, at least Peter, had correctly perceived the identity of Jesus. Jesus was not Jeremiah, not Isaiah, and not Elijah. Rather, Jesus was the Christ. This powerful insight had yet to grow to its fullest meaning and application. The disciples saw Jesus as the Anointed King but had yet to understand the secrets of his glory and his kingdom (8:31–33). Jesus asked them to tell no one that he was the Christ and then forewarned them of his coming death.

Revealing the Cross (8:31–33)

Jesus added to the disciples' understanding by teaching them about the coming crucifixion and resurrection. "He spoke plainly about this" (8:32). The tense of the verb may indicate that he kept on speaking to them of his suffering. Peter's response may have come immediately or after several hours or days of listening to the Master.

Lesson in a Rubber Band

Studying under T. B. Maston was one of my great joys. He would often illustrate a life philosophy with a rubber band. If the band was without tension, it was useless. If it had too much tension, it would break and cause great pain. Stretched to the right proportion, the constructive tension made the rubber band useful.

Similarly, testing puts tension on us and is the major reason we grow, learn, perform, and extend ourselves. Testing provides opportunity for creativity and resourcefulness. How have times of testing changed your life?

Jesus taught them that he "must suffer many things" (8:31). The word "must" expresses moral and spiritual necessity and should be applied to all of the following verbs, as "must be rejected," "must be killed," and "must rise again." "Rejected" means "to put to the test in order to throw out." Jesus described the process and named the Jewish religious leaders—"the elders, chief priests and teachers of the law"—who would test him and reject him (8:31). Jesus was not the kind of Messiah they expected or wanted.

Not only must the disciples accept the coming fact of Jesus' crucifixion, they must be prepared to accept their own cross.

Peter had heard enough. Overwhelmed by Jesus' prophesy of pain, rejection, and death, Peter took Jesus aside "and began to rebuke him" (8:32). "Rebuke" has the sense of censure, reprimand, and criticism in order to turn back. Peter's compassion for Christ makes the rebuke natural and expected. Peter found the words of Jesus mystifying, revolting, and shocking. How could Jesus accomplish his goals if he were dead? Peter called on Jesus to think of himself and to turn back and spare himself such treatment and abuse. Jesus was greatly disturbed on hearing these thoughts from the mouth of one he had chosen.

The same word used for Peter's "rebuke" of Jesus is used of Jesus as Jesus "rebuked" Peter and Satan (8:33). Jesus quickly and intensely turned with stinging force to say (8:33), "Get behind me, Satan!" Jesus recognized the temptation of Satan here at this strategic moment just as Jesus had experienced it at the crucial time when he began his earthly ministry (1:12–13). Peter was a pawn of Satan who sought again to tempt Christ to give up the spiritual kingdom for the earthly one.

A crucial turning point in the ministry of Jesus was taking place.

Jesus immediately recognized the source of the temptation and responded to Peter, "'You do not have in mind the things of God, but the things of men'" (8:33). Jesus was telling Peter that he had missed the point and still had much to learn before he grasped the deeper meaning of who Jesus was and what Jesus was doing.

Revealing the Commitment (8:34–38)

Not only must the disciples accept the coming fact of Jesus' crucifixion, they must be prepared to accept their own cross. The cross that Peter rejected for Christ must now be his own. Christ included the crowd and said, "If anyone would come after me, he must deny himself and take up his cross and follow me" (8:34).

The verbs translated "deny" and "take up" are both the same tense and express acts that are once for all. The tense of the verb translated "follow" means habitual and continuous action. Christians are to deny themselves and take up the cross once for all as a determined lifestyle and then to keep on following.

Revealing the Cost (8:35–37)

With a play on words that must have seemed more like a riddle, Jesus went to the bottom line and stated the underlying principle of cross-taking: "For whoever wants to save his life will lose it, but whoever

Taking Up One's Cross

Christ invoked the imagery of the sentenced offender bearing his own cross to the place of death. The metaphor was vague to the disciples and to us today.

One's "cross" is not some hardship or handicap to bear, some suffering to endure, or some unfortunate experience to go through such as an illness, vocational loss, ungrateful spouse, or rebellious child. Rather, the Christian's cross is an act of the will of choosing Christ regardless of the cost. It is giving up our wants for Christ's will, our rewards for Christ's righteousness, our liberty for Christ's Lordship.

The cross-taking Christian is to carry out the Great Commission even if it means humiliation, shame, rejection, debasement, and personal sacrifice. No cross can be carried without self-denial, but no single denial or sacrifice can be equated with carrying one's cross. The cross is a way of life, not merely a single act of living.

loses his life for me and for the gospel will save it" (8:35). This is the heart and soul of the Christian faith.

Jesus here appealed to the basic human hunger to "save" one's life. The only way to save one's life is to give oneself away for sake of the gospel and thus to "lose it." Losing one's life for the sake of the gospel will accomplish far more than clinging to one's own personal selfish ambitions. Saving one's life for the here and now will mean losing one's life in eternity. One gains the best by losing the least, for the rewards of this world are not ultimately satisfying. Jesus had given them a radical vision and told them what it would cost to achieve it. The high calling of life is "for [Jesus] and for the gospel" (8:35).

Losing one's life for the sake of the gospel will accomplish far more than clinging to one's own personal selfish ambitions.

To help in a deeper understanding of the principle, Jesus continued by asking, "What good is it for a man to gain the whole world, yet forfeit his soul? Or what will a man give in exchange for his soul?" (8:36–37) Jesus showed he understands the heart of human nature by asking where one puts value and worth. Will a person live his or her life for cheap successes of pleasure, position, production, profit, or popularity? Living for these kinds of values is not a bargain but a cheap bag of tricks. Gaining the whole world is not worth a single soul.

Revealing the Challenge (8:38)

Jesus connected the choice of saving and losing one's life with the emotion of shame or embarrassment. Anticipating the response of the crowd to his message, Jesus warned them emphatically, "If anyone is ashamed of me and my words in this adulterous and sinful generation, the Son of Man will be ashamed of him when he comes in his Father's glory with the holy angels" (8:38). Jesus apparently expected the masses to be embarrassed over his manner of life, his teachings, and his death.

Often people will hear the gospel, consider taking the step of faith, but refuse to do so because of embarrassment about "walking the aisle," being baptized, or letting their friends know.

Shame is very powerful. It has both a positive and a negative consequence. Positively, it can be the feeling that indicates one's relationship with God, having a sense of divine judgment following from guilt. Shame encourages repentance and seeks forgiveness. Negatively, this same feeling can be one of failure and rejection caused by embarrassment. Shame is the intense feeling of inferiority and humiliation that comes from disgrace or censure. Acceptance is such a human need that embarrassment becomes its pawn. Often people will hear the gospel, consider taking the step of faith, but refuse to do so because of embarrassment about "walking the aisle," being baptized, or letting their friends know. Such a sense of shame becomes the devil's snare and the bondage of the soul.

The feeling of embarrassment hinders and impedes the cause of Christ and creates doubt and perplexity. Satan will use the force of shame and embarrassment to restrict and restrain people Christ calls to be his disciples. Jesus sees shame and embarrassment as a major human hurdle to overcome. The Apostle Paul countered, "I am not ashamed of the gospel because it is the power of God for the salvation of everyone who believes: first for the Jew, then for the Gentile" (Romans 1:16)

QUESTIONS

1. What is the relationship of Messiahship and discipleship?

2. Why do you think Peter got Jesus' title correct but did not understand the cross?

3. If following Christ doesn't cost you something, is it worth doing? What has following Christ cost you?

4. How has your faith been tested lately? Is there power in testing?

5. Why is this experience of testing called a turning point in the life of Jesus? Do you think that the setting for Jesus' questions was coincidental or planned?

6. Do any people you know have any difficulty identifying Jesus as the Christ? Why?

NOTES

1. "China's Christian Underground," *U. S. News and World Report* (April 30, 2001).

UNIT

THREE

Suffering for Us

When Jimmy Carter was President of the United States, he invited my wife and me to join other church leaders for a memorable event at the White House. After an elegant meal, we went into the East Room for a private performance of a Broadway hit show. The show had experienced months of spectacular success before sell-out crowds in London. Now the performance was playing to overflow audiences on Broadway. The performance was titled, *The Gospel of Mark.* Alec McGowan, a British actor, stood on an empty stage. With a few words of introduction, for several hours he quoted from memory the King James Version of the Gospel of Mark. Nothing was added. What we heard was directly from the pages of the English Bible.

The experience was spellbinding. I had read the gospel, studied it, translated it, and preached from it, but I had never experienced it as though it were

Mark himself telling the story. The audience, made up I'm sure of both believers and skeptics, was gripped with the drama. We felt the excitement of the miracles, heard the clarity of Jesus' teachings, and experienced the anticipation as Jesus approached Jerusalem. We were touched by the heartbreaking shock of Jesus' death and burial. Then we almost applauded at the glorious announcement of the resurrection. I went back home promising never to present the gospel in a dull or routine manner. The gospel is indeed good news.

So, as we come to this closing unit in our study of Mark, I hope you too will be gripped by the drama of the greatest story ever told.

You will note that this unit contains a "bonus" lesson. This extra lesson on Mark 13 is included because of the importance of the teachings of this chapter and the need to provide help in understanding its meaning in context. It is included as an extra lesson rather than a numbered lesson in order to give classes the choice of when and how to study it. Furthermore, including Mark 13 as an extra lesson provides the opportunity to study the events surrounding Jesus' crucifixion more fully in the numbered lessons.

Unit 3: Suffering for Us

UNIT THREE, SUFFERING FOR US

Lesson 9	Jesus Teaches About Service	Mark 9:33–37; 10:35–45
Lesson 10	Jesus Asserts His Authority	Mark 11:15–18, 27—12:12
Bonus Lesson	Jesus Teaches About the Future	Mark 13:1–37
Lesson 11	Jesus Gives His Life	Mark 14:12–26, 32–42
Lesson 12	Jesus Is Condemned	Mark 14:53—15:20
Lesson 13	Jesus Dies and Lives Again!	Mark 15:21–41; 16:1–8

LESSON NINE

Jesus Teaches About Service

Focal Text

Mark 9:30–37; 10:35–45

Background

Mark 9:1—10:52

Main Idea

Jesus teaches his disciples that greatness comes only through the kind of humble service exemplified supremely by Jesus himself.

Question to Explore

What makes a person truly great?

Study Aim

To evaluate my life by the standard Jesus set for greatness

Study and Action Emphases

- Minister to human needs in the name of Jesus Christ
- Equip people for ministry in the church and in the world
- Develop Christian families
- Strengthen existing churches and start new congregations

Quick Read

Responding to his disciples' repeated wrangling over rank, Jesus focused attention on a little child to teach them that true greatness is found in humble service and self-giving sacrifice.

In Arlington, Texas, sponsored by the First Baptist Church, is a remarkable ministry called, "Mission Arlington." For fifteen years, Tillie Burgin, the director, has worked long hours every day feeding, clothing, and sheltering not just the homeless, but anyone in need. Every day, Mission Arlington provides more than 200 families with meals, clothing, transportation, counseling, medical aid, Bible study, worship, and financial assistance.

Because of her selfless service to the marginal and neglected, President George W. Bush once compared "Miss Tillie" to Mother Teresa. She was recently inducted into the Texas Women's Hall of Fame and has an Arlington elementary school named for her. Such recognition embarrasses the former missionary to Korea, because one of her most striking qualities is humility. She exemplifies Jesus' teaching that true greatness is found in serving others (Mark 9:30–37).

Scene One: The Journey to Capernaum (9:30–37)

The background passage, Mark 9:1—10:52, provides the setting for our focal text. Mark 9:1–13 records the dazzling transformation of Jesus on a mountain (tradition says it was Mt. Tabor) with Peter, James, and John. Joining the others at the foot of the mountain, they encountered a distraught father with a demon-possessed son whom the disciples could not heal. Jesus rebuked the demon and healed the boy

Mark 9:30–37

30They went on from there and passed through Galilee.
He did not want anyone to know it; 31for he was teaching
his disciples, saying to them, "The Son of Man is to be
betrayed into human hands, and they will kill him, and
three days after being killed, he will rise again." 32But
they did not understand what he was saying and were
afraid to ask him.

33Then they came to Capernaum; and when he was in
the house he asked them, "What were you arguing
about on the way?" 34But they were silent, for on the way
they had argued with one another who was the greatest.
35He sat down, called the twelve, and said to them,
"Whoever wants to be first must be last of all and servant
of all." 36Then he took a little child and put it among
them; and taking it in his arms, he said to them, 37"Who-
ever welcomes one such child in my name welcomes
me, and whoever welcomes me welcomes not me but
the one who sent me."

Mark 10:35–45

35James and John, the sons of Zebedee, came forward
to him and said to him, "Teacher, we want you to do for
us whatever we ask of you." 36And he said to them,
"What is it you want me to do for you?" 37And they said
to him, "Grant us to sit, one at your right hand and one
at your left, in your glory." 38But Jesus said to them, "You

do not know what you are asking. Are you able to drink
the cup that I drink, or be baptized with the baptism that
I am baptized with?" 39They replied, "We are able." Then
Jesus said to them, "The cup that I drink you will drink;
and with the baptism with which I am baptized, you will
be baptized; 40but to sit at my right hand or at my left is
not mine to grant, but it is for those for whom it has
been prepared."

41When the ten heard this, they began to be angry with
James and John. 42So Jesus called them and said to them,
"You know that among the Gentiles those whom they
recognize as their rulers lord it over them, and their great
ones are tyrants over them. 43But it is not so among you;
but whoever wishes to become great among you must
be your servant, 44and whoever wishes to be first among
you must be slave of all. 45For the Son of Man came not
to be served but to serve, and to give his life a ransom
for many."

(9:14–29). Following this miracle, our focal text picks up the story on the road from the mountain to Capernaum. In addition to the passages we will study in the focal text, Mark reports an encounter with an anonymous exorcist (9:38–41), instructions on discipline, marriage, and children (9:42—10:16), an encounter with the rich young ruler (10:17–31), and the healing of Bartimaeus (10:46–52).

1. Disclosure: Jesus predicts his death (9:30–32). Some suggest that Mark inserted this detailed description of

Jesus' suffering after the fact, making it appear Jesus had predicted the events. Others explain that based on his earlier conflicts with religious leaders, Jesus simply "put two and two together" and, using his common sense, anticipated what would likely happen. But the Bible clearly states that Jesus employed supernatural foresight, and these detailed predictions reflect his miraculous deity.

> *We should always ask,* Would I do this if Jesus were here watching and listening?

The verbs translated "teaching" and "saying," (9:31) indicate continuous action. Jesus kept on predicting his crucifixion, "but they did not understand" (9:32). Mark says they were afraid to ask for clarification. Why? Perhaps they suspected the explanation would be more bad news, and they refused to hear it. Or maybe they remembered how Jesus rebuked Simon Peter for his response to a similar prediction in Mark 8:32. Silence seemed safer.

2. Exposure: Jesus chides their self-centered wrangling (9:33–34). The house in verse 33 was undoubtedly the house of Simon Peter. Still today, travelers to Capernaum are shown the excavated foundations of a first-century house that archeologists identify as Peter's house.

Once inside, Jesus casually inquired (9:33), "'What were you arguing about on the way?'" Remember, the Lord could foresee the details of his death in Jerusalem, and so he already knew the content of their discussions. He was not asking to get information but to expose their pathetic wrangling. Mark tells us they said nothing. They had been debating who was the greatest, and they were embarrassed (9:34).

As long as Jesus hadn't heard their dispute, it didn't seem so bad, but now that he knew, they were ashamed. How many of our actions that seem innocent at the time, would be embarrassing if Jesus were watching? Actually, Jesus *is* watching. He knows everything we do and say. We should always ask, *Would I do this if Jesus were here watching and listening?*

The way to true greatness involves two steps: "last of all and servant of all" (9:35).

We condemn these two disciples, but the church still has people like James and John, go-getters and status-seekers who hinder God's work by scrapping for preeminence. In 1265 Kublai Kahn ruled the Mongol Empire stretching from the Black Sea to the Pacific Ocean. He sent Marco Polo back to ask the Church in Rome to send 100 missionaries to teach Christianity in his court. But church leaders were so busy competing among themselves for positions of power that they did not respond for twenty-eight years. Then they sent out only one missionary. Kublai Kahn, already retired, said, "It is too late. I have grown old in my idolatry."

3. Nurture: Jesus helps the disciples understand true greatness (9:35–37). Sitting was the usual posture of a Jewish teacher (see Matthew 5:1; Luke 5:3; John 8:2). By sitting down, Jesus signaled he was about to say something very important.

Notice, Jesus didn't condemn their desire to be great in God's kingdom. Instead, Jesus corrected their faulty view of greatness and how to attain it. The way to true greatness involves two steps: "last of all and servant of all" (9:35).

These two steps are not the same. Being "last of all" describes an attitude of humility. Being "servant of all" describes unselfish ministry action. Each is essential to the other. It's possible to be humble (last of all), but be lazy and refuse to serve others. On the other hand, it's possible to minister to others without being truly humble. I've known preachers who were self-effacing and humble, but, remaining comfortably secluded, they withdrew from needy people. Equally misguided are those who help the needy, but want everybody to notice what they do and brag on them. Neither humility without service nor service without humility is the way to greatness. Jesus explained you must be both "last of all" and "servant of all."

Disciples who desire true greatness should pay attention to ordinary, insignificant people who are weak, who have no wealth, influence, or power.

As he often did, Jesus employed a visual aid—a little child in this case—to reinforce the lesson. Since this incident took place in the house of Simon Peter, the child was likely his. The child was old enough to stand by the side of Jesus (see Luke 9:47), and small enough to sit on Jesus' lap and be embraced. Imagine the look of wonder in the eyes of the little child. Since the Gospel of Mark is based on Simon Peter's experiences with Jesus, we assume he shared with Mark the precious memory of his little child in the arms of Jesus.

The child represented the twin steps to greatness, being " last of all" (humility) and being "servant of all" (ministry). First, a child symbolized humility, especially in the ancient world where children were low on the scale of significance. In fact, the Aramaic word for child is the same as the word for servant. A child is

The Cup

Jesus used the cup and baptism to symbolize suffering and death. Chrysostom, a fourth-century church leader, suggested two reasons Jesus used baptism to symbolize death. First, because by Jesus' death, he cleansed the world. Second, because of the ease with which Jesus would rise again. One who is baptized in water easily rises up because the water in which he is immersed poses no hindrance. So, Christ rose with ease since the grave could not hinder him.[2]

Jesus predicted that James and John would indeed drink suffering's cup and endure death's baptism. Jesus was right. James was beheaded by Herod Agrippa I in AD 44. John endured a slower martyrdom, exiled on lonely Patmos. Jesus said, "To the one who conquers I will give a place with me on my throne" (Revelation 3:21). So the two disciples did eventually attain their seats at the Master's side. But the path was not what they expected, and the real thrones were more glorious than they ever dreamed.

unpretentious, unsophisticated, with a natural disregard for social rank. A king's child has no more innate thoughts of self-greatness than a beggar's child. So humility was what Jesus encouraged the disciples to emulate. Instead of arguing over who was the greatest, they needed to be child-like, not king-like.

Paul gave similar advice when he wrote: "I say to everyone among you not to think of yourself more highly than you ought to think . . . outdo one another in showing honor" (Romans 12:3, 10). In addition, Paul instructed, "In humility, regard others as better than yourselves" (Philippians 2:3).

> *In God's house, no one is to be regarded as either a kingpin or a nonentity.*

But the child on Jesus' lap so far only represented humility. What about ministry, the second step to greatness? To illustrate this step, Jesus lifted the child up and embraced him, demonstrating what it means to be "the servant of all." Jesus said, "Whosoever welcomes one such child in my name welcomes me" (9:37). Jesus was showing that the kind of people we ought to serve are like the child: people who have no influence, people who can't give us anything or enhance our prestige. Disciples who desire true greatness should pay attention to ordinary, insignificant people who are weak, who have no wealth, influence, or power. If we serve people like that, Jesus said, we are serving him and the Father.

Maybe James remembered this lesson when he wrote, "For if a person with gold rings and in fine clothes comes into your assembly, and if a poor person in dirty clothes also comes in, and if you take notice of the one wearing the fine clothes and say, 'Have a seat here, please,' while to the one who is poor you say, 'Stand there,' or, 'Sit at my feet,' have you not made distinctions among yourselves, and become judges with evil thoughts?" (James 2:2–4). In God's house, no one is to be regarded as either a kingpin or a nonentity.

Tillie Burgin, the director of Mission Arlington described at the beginning of the lesson, personifies the kind of service Jesus described. One of her volunteers said, "She is truly humble, never asking us to do anything she hasn't already done. If the dumpster topples over, she's out there picking it up. Once you've seen her sweeping up the alley a few hundred times, you kind of want to help." The mission is open 365 days a year ministering to the needy. Miss Tillie is there every day before dawn and doesn't leave until 9 p.m. The mission closes early only on Christmas day, but her son says, even then, when she closes up she says, "What if we miss somebody?"[1]

This is how we attain true greatness according to Jesus: by humility (being the last of all) and by selfless ministry (being the servant of all).

Scene Two: The Journey to Jerusalem (10:32–45)

1. Another miraculous prediction (10:32–34). Jesus and the disciples began their final trip to Jerusalem. Along the way, for the third time and with greater detail, Jesus solemnly predicted the future. When Jesus and the disciples arrived in the great city, he would be betrayed, condemned, mocked, spit upon, scourged, and killed (10:32–34). And, like the other two predictions, Jesus' words sailed right over their heads—in one ear and out the other. Jesus was marching to his death, and the straggling disciples were pushing and shoving, trying to establish the order of the procession behind him.

2. Another selfish request (10:35–37). Peter, James, and John were closest to Jesus, in the "inner circle," often with him at crucial events. Now two of them, James and John, tried to draw the inner circle a little tighter. Leaving Simon Peter out, they deviously tried to maneuver themselves into the places of honor with Jesus. They wanted to be at Jesus' right hand and left hand, co-rulers with him. Assuming they had the inside track since their mother, Salome, was the sister to Mary, Jesus' mother, they even persuaded "Aunt Salome" to join their presumptuous request for prominence (see Mark 15:40; Matthew 20:20; 27:56).

Here was Jesus, talking about all he was about to do, and here were James and John with a shopping list of all they wanted to get.

No wonder the other disciples were indignant (Mark 10:41). Here was Jesus, talking about all he was about to do, and here were James and John with a shopping list of all they wanted to get. But it was not their insensitive request that made the other disciples mad. They were angry at James and John for getting the jump on them, claiming the two positions of power before the rest had a chance to promote themselves.

Jesus responded gently, never condemning their desire for greatness in his kingdom but realizing their motives were mixed. Their quest for greatness was not altogether bad, but rather a blending of pride and love.

Scholars believe that the Taj Mahal, the mausoleum in India built by Shah Jahan about 1631–33, is not necessarily the beautiful monument to love, marital devotion, and bereavement often assumed. Ancient records reveal that Shah Jahan was arrogant, petty, ruthless, incestuous, and unfaithful to his wife. The inscriptions from the Koran he inscribed on the walls of the building were a vainglorious attempt to control and rival God. The monument is actually a memorial to love and pride mixed together.

In a similar fashion, the disciples' request was a mixture of love and pride. Give James and John credit. They did love Jesus. They believed in Jesus. They wanted to be with Jesus. James and John truly expected their itinerant Teacher, the humble Carpenter from Nazareth, to overthrow the Roman occupation. With one word, Jesus would annihilate the soldiers stationed at Fort Antonia, expel the Roman procurator, Pontius Pilate, and dethrone King Herod. Then after recruiting an army of young Jewish soldiers, Jesus would free all the Jews and reign in Herod's palace as King Jesus.

On Wanting to Be Praised

If a person reaches out to help others, but wants to be praised for it, has that person met the requirement Jesus gave for true greatness? If not, what's missing?

This is the scenario James and John envisioned. It took enormous faith to believe it and enormous courage to accept the danger such a dream entailed. So Jesus didn't rebuke them for wanting to share his ultimate victory. Instead, Jesus corrected their false conceptions of what lay ahead and taught them about true greatness and how to attain it.

3. Another lesson on true greatness (10:38–45). First, Jesus warned them about the suffering they would encounter if their request to be at his right and left were granted. Surely the Lord had to restrain his dismay at their naïve lack of understanding. If Jesus granted their petition literally, to be on his right and left in Jerusalem, the sons of Zebedee would end up on the crosses to Jesus' right and left at Golgotha. The only other time the terms "right" and "left" are used together in Mark's Gospel is at the crucifixion where two bandits died on crosses beside him (Mark 15:27). Crosses were not the thrones James and John had in mind when they said they could drink the cup and go through the baptism with Jesus.

Second, contrasting true greatness with the world's idea, Jesus defined the kind of greatness they should strive for (10:42–44). It is not the imperial greatness typical of the pagan world. In the worldly realm, the higher a person ranks, the more that person is served. But in the heavenly realm, the higher a person ranks, the more that person serves others.

Jesus says your desire to be great is acceptable, but to attain true greatness you must, like Jesus, become a servant, a slave, and a sacrificer.

According to Jesus, to attain true greatness, a person must take three steps. The steps are similar to the two steps (humility and ministry) discussed previously. In 10:43–45, Jesus used three Greek words beginning with the letter "D"—*diakonos, doulos, and dounai*. They refer to being a servant, a slave, and a sacrificer. If you want to be great in the eyes of Jesus, you must be willing: (1) to minister to others as a servant—*diakonos*; (2) to surrender to God as a slave—*doulos*; and (3) to give your life as a sacrificer—*dounai*. (*Dounai* is the word from which we get the English word "donor.")

Jesus then reinforced the lesson with a supreme example (10:45). Jesus himself ("the Son of Man") became:

(1) a servant, coming not to be served, but to serve (He washed the disciples' feet. See John 13:1–5.)

(2) a slave, obeying the will of the Father ("Father . . . not what I want, but what you want." See Mark 14:36.)

(3) a sacrificer, dying as a ransom for sinners. (Mark's only explanation of why Jesus died. See Mark 10:45.)

Taking these steps, Jesus became truly great—King of Kings and Lord of Lords. Do you want to really be somebody as a Christian? Jesus says your desire to be great is acceptable, but to attain true greatness you must, like Jesus, become a servant, a slave, and a sacrificer.

QUESTIONS

1. How legitimate is it for Christians to desire greatness in their work for Christ?

2. How practical in today's competitive world is Jesus' teaching about putting yourself last?

3. What is there about children that caused Jesus to use them so often as examples of what we should be?

4. Why did the disciples have such difficulty understanding Jesus' frequent predictions about his death?

NOTES

1. *Fort Worth Star Telegram*, April 12, 2000, page 9E.
2. Thomas C. Oden, ed., *Ancient Christian Commentary on Scripture: Mark,* (Downers Grove: Intervarsity Press, 1998), 151.

LESSON TEN

Jesus Asserts His Authority

Focal Text

Mark 11:15–18, 27—12:12

Background

Mark 11:1—12:44

Main Idea

Jesus' actions and his teachings demonstrated his authority as the Son of God.

Question to Explore

Who's in charge here?

Study Aim

To identify implications for life of Jesus' demonstration of his authority through his actions and his teachings

Study and Action Emphases

- Share the gospel of Jesus Christ with all people
- Equip people for ministry in the church and in the world

Quick Read

Arriving in Jerusalem a few days before his crucifixion, Jesus asserted his authority by condemning a fig tree, cleansing the temple, answering his critics, and avoiding arrest.

During the national crisis following the 1981 assassination attempt on President Ronald Reagan, the White House staff was in disarray. Caught off guard, various spokespeople tried to assure the American people that everything was under control. Alexander Haig, Secretary of State, confused the issue when he boldly claimed on television, "I'm in charge here." Actually, the order of succession in the event of the incapacity of both the President and Vice President goes to the Speaker of the House, the President of the Senate, and *then* the Secretary of State. Haig claimed to be in charge, but he wasn't.

As Jesus led his disciples to Jerusalem, he obviously was in charge. There was no aimless wandering, no hesitation. Jesus marched forward, directing the drama of his sacrificial death and ultimate resurrection. In Mark 11—12, the background passage, we see Jesus asserting his authority in an amazing series of actions.

The First Assertion of Jesus' Authority: the Entry into Jerusalem (11:1–10)

Leaving Bethany early in the morning, Jesus was accompanied by a large group of people from Bethany. Encouraged by the raising of Lazarus from the dead (John 11), they hoped Jesus would perform even greater miracles in Jerusalem where 250,000 Passover visitors had swelled the population to almost a half million. Up the eastern slope of the Mount of

Mark 11:15–18, 27–33

15 Then they came to Jerusalem. And he entered the
temple and began to drive out those who were selling
and those who were buying in the temple, and he over-
turned the tables of the money changers and the seats of
those who sold doves; 16 and he would not allow anyone
to carry anything through the temple. 17 He was teaching
and saying, "Is it not written,

'My house shall be called a house of prayer for all the
nations'?

But you have made it a den of robbers."

18 And when the chief priests and the scribes heard it, they
kept looking for a way to kill him; for they were afraid of
him, because the whole crowd was spellbound by his
teaching. 19 And when evening came, Jesus and his disci-
ples went out of the city.

● ●

27 Again they came to Jerusalem. As he was walking in
the temple, the chief priests, the scribes, and the elders
came to him 28 and said, "By what authority are you
doing these things? Who gave you this authority to do
them?" 29 Jesus said to them, "I will ask you one question;
answer me, and I will tell you by what authority I do
these things. 30 Did the baptism of John come from
heaven, or was it of human origin? Answer me." 31 They
argued with one another, "If we say, 'From heaven,' he
will say, 'Why then did you not believe him?' 32 But shall

we say, 'Of human origin'?"—they were afraid of the crowd, for all regarded John as truly a prophet. 33 So they answered Jesus, "We do not know." And Jesus said to them, "Neither will I tell you by what authority I am doing these things."

Mark 12:1–12

1 Then he began to speak to them in parables. "A man planted a vineyard, put a fence around it, dug a pit for the wine press, and built a watchtower; then he leased it to tenants and went to another country. 2 When the season came, he sent a slave to the tenants to collect from them his share of the produce of the vineyard. 3 But they seized him, and beat him, and sent him away empty-handed. 4 And again he sent another slave to them; this one they beat over the head and insulted. 5 Then he sent another, and that one they killed. And so it was with many others; some they beat, and others they killed. 6 He had still one other, a beloved son. Finally he sent him to them, saying, 'They will respect my son.' 7 But those tenants said to one another, 'This is the heir; come, let us kill him, and the inheritance will be ours.' 8 So they seized him, killed him, and threw him out of the vineyard. 9 What then will the owner of the vineyard do? He will come and destroy the tenants and give the vineyard to others. 10 Have you not read this scripture:

> 'The stone that the builders rejected
> has become the cornerstone;

> 11 this was the Lord's doing,
> and it is amazing in our eyes'?"
> 12 When they realized that he had told this parable against them, they wanted to arrest him, but they feared the crowd. So they left him and went away.

Olives they traveled to the little village of Bethphage. Here the entourage from Bethany met another even larger group coming from Jerusalem with the disciples bringing the donkey Jesus would ride.

Jesus mounted the donkey, and the procession climbed over the crest of Olivet with its dramatic view of Jerusalem. The procession continued down the western slope into the Valley of Kidron to the Beautiful Gate of Jerusalem. Entering the city, the people waved their palm branches and lay their cloaks in front of Jesus, shouting (Mark 11:10), "Blessed is the coming kingdom of our father David; Hosanna in the highest!" After a brief inspection of the temple and the city, Jesus returned to Bethany.

Until now, the Lord had forbidden any public recognition of his kingship, but here he encouraged those who hailed him—a King on a borrowed donkey. Jesus usually dampened the people's smoldering enthusiasm, but he now fanned it into a crackling flame. Every token of royal honor Jesus accepted was a challenge to his enemies. Every hosanna drove that challenge home. Why this change? Because now Jesus' hour *had* come. Jesus was ready to proclaim his kingship and finish his task. Who's in charge here?

Jesus is, directing every act in the final drama. If anyone doubts that Jesus claimed to be the Messiah, here is striking evidence that he did.

The Second Assertion of Jesus' Authority: the Miraculous Condemnation of the Fig Tree (11:12–14, 20–23)

After spending Sunday night back in Bethany, Jesus made his second trip into Jerusalem. It was Monday. Somewhere along the road, the group stopped at one of the many fig trees that dotted the mountain slopes. Mark explains that Jesus was hungry and wanted to see whether the tree had any figs. But since it was not the season for fruit, the tree had only leaves. Jesus spoke to the tree in righteous judgment. On the visit to Jerusalem the next day, the tree had withered to its roots (11:20).

As Jesus led his disciples to Jerusalem, he obviously was in charge.

Why would Jesus curse a tree for not bearing fruit out of season? Jesus never used his miraculous powers to meet his own needs. For example, Jesus refused to turn the stones to bread when he was hungry (Matthew 4: 3–4). Thus, it seems unlikely Jesus would be angry at an innocent tree for not providing his lunch! This puzzling detail should lead the reader to assume there is something deeper here beyond the surface event. Another clue that something else is going on is the fact that the incident of the leafy tree is divided into two parts, "sandwiching" the story of moneychangers in the temple (see the discussion of "bracketing" in the sidebar).

Each of these two accounts interprets the other. By cursing the fig tree, Jesus dramatized the barrenness of current religious life in Israel. Later, Jesus' actions in the temple carried out the same theme—outrage at the fruitlessness of temple worship. The barren fig tree was like barren temple worship—empty, shallow, its rituals unable to prepare people for the coming Messiah. Like the tree, Israel appeared to be thriving, but the appearance was deceiving. Like the fig tree, Israel was all leaves and no fruit.

This theme is repeated in the parable of the vineyard (Mark 12:1–11). Just as Jesus looked for fruit on the tree, so God, the owner of the vineyard, looked for harvest from the vineyard. When there was no harvest, the tenants were destroyed and the vineyard given away.

The Third Assertion of Jesus' Authority: the Driving Out of the Moneychangers (11:15–18)

On Sunday of Jesus' last week, he entered Jerusalem to the cheers of the crowd. Mark tells us that he then walked into the temple "and when he had looked around at everything, as it was already late, he went

Bracketing or Sandwiching

Mark 11:12–22 is an example of a literary technique called *bracketing, sandwiching,* or *intercalation*. Mark's account of the driving out of the merchants in the temple is *sandwiched* between two parts of his story of the fig tree. Notice the fig tree incident begins in verse 12 and picks up again in verse 20. In between these two "brackets" is Mark's description of the cleansing of the temple (11:15–19).

This is the pattern:

FIG TREE	[CLEANSING OF THE TEMPLE]	FIG TREE
(11:12–14)	(11:15–19)	(11:20–22)

Mark used this technique regularly. (Compare Mark 3:20–21; 3:22–30; 3:31–35.) Each of the two narratives helps us understand the other.

The cursing of the fig tree and the expulsion of the merchants from the temple are dramatic actions symbolizing the same thing: a condemnation of Israel's religion, particularly, the empty ceremonial worship in the temple. Jesus was acting out this condemnation in the same way Old Testament prophets did. For example, Isaiah went barefoot and without clothes to symbolize the stripping of Egypt (Isaiah 20:1–6). Jeremiah wore a wooden yoke around his neck to symbolize the future enslavement to the king of Babylon (Jeremiah 27:1–15; 28:10–17).

out to Bethany" (11:11). The next day, Jesus and the disciples returned to the temple, walking down the Roman street toward the grand stairway entrance.

Part of that road is still visible just below the ruins of the Western Wall. This broad entryway to the temple had become a public market place. Some believe the incident took place in the temple court of Gentiles, but it appears more likely that it was on the huge staircase and *stoa* (porch) leading into the court.

The temple of Solomon had been destroyed by the Babylonians in 586 BC. Some seventy years later, Zerrubbabel had rebuilt a smaller temple. Zerubbabel's temple was then replaced by Herod's magnificent structure. Begun in 20–19 BC, it took ten years to complete the main building, and the entire complex was not completed until AD 64, just six years before its total destruction. So during Jesus' day, the temple and outer courts encompassed about thirty-five acres and was still under construction. The lavishly restored temple, a world-renowned wonder, had become synonymous with the nation.

Jesus usually dampened the people's smoldering enthusiasm, but he now fanned it into a crackling flame.

Crowding the stairs and the portico leading into the outer court, and perhaps spilling over into the courtyard itself, were noisy merchants selling cattle, sheep, doves, and pigeons for use as sacrifices. Since the sacrificial animal had to be perfect, without blemish, worshippers usually did not risk bringing their own from home, lest the animal be injured on the way. Instead, the worshippers purchased unblemished sacrifices at the temple entrance. In addition, the regular

Roman *denarii* (the dollar of that day) bore the image of Caesar and therefore violated the Jewish prohibition of graven images. So worshippers had to change their Roman money for temple shekels.

Imagine the scene, with bellowing animals, hawking merchants, and jingling coins. It has been described as a Judean version of London's Hyde Park, with street-corner preachers, lecturers, priests, soldiers, and children, along with beggars and Gentiles from distant places. The temple steps were *the* experience in Jerusalem.

With surprising and uncharacteristic ferocity, Jesus began to drive out the merchants and moneychangers, turning over their tables and seats. Jesus then turned back any who tried to carry vessels or other paraphernalia through the temple as a short cut. "'Is it not written, 'My house shall be called a house of prayer for all the nations? But you have made it a den of robbers'" (11:17).

> *. . . Jesus was upset because the temple had become a refuge, a den, for people who robbed widows' houses and then self-righteously came to the temple to perform the rituals of worship in safety.*

What was Jesus doing? Some say he was attempting to arouse opposition, intentionally setting the spark that would ignite an armed revolt. Others say he was condemning the flagrant abuses, trying to reform temple worship and make room for those who had been displaced by the merchants. This explanation lies behind the popular designation of this event as *the cleansing of the temple*. But this action probably took place at the public entrance of the temple, not in the area of worship. If cleansing the temple had been Jesus' purpose, the cleansing didn't last long. The moneychangers and merchants soon picked up their coins, herded up their animals, and resumed the same practice. Furthermore, why would Jesus try to reform or purify something he predicted without any great anguish would soon be destroyed (13:1–2)? What was Jesus doing?

Perhaps a better explanation is that Jesus did not intend to reform temple worship. Like other prophets who sometimes acted out their sermons, Jesus was dramatizing God's rejection of temple worship and its coming destruction. Jesus was making a point rather than trying to change things in the temple. He was attacking the very heart of the temple's existence—the money, the sacrifices, the sacred vessels carried in worship. Jesus was not trying to reform temple worship; rather, Jesus was heralding its abolition.

Quoting Jeremiah 7:11 about the temple, Jesus charged, "You have made it a den of robbers" (Mark 11:17). Jesus was not berating the dishonesty of the merchants. Remember, Jesus drove out both the sellers *and* the buyers. Furthermore, a den is where the robber hides *after* he has stolen. A better interpretation is that Jesus was upset because the temple had become a refuge, a den, for people who robbed widows' houses and then self-righteously came to the temple to perform the rituals of worship in safety.

Quoting Isaiah 56:7, Jesus said that God intended the temple to be a "house of prayer for all the nations"

(Mark 11:17). In saying this, Jesus was rejecting the popular idea that the temple was a national shrine exclusively for Israel. Instead, God intended it to be a place where outcasts and foreigners from all nations could learn to worship him. As it was, the temple divided Israel from the nations.

Salvation would no longer be provided through the blood of animals, but through the ultimate sacrifice, once for all, of the Lamb of God.

The incident of the leafy tree that bore no fruit, which brackets the story of the temple, reinforces this interpretation. Just as the tree would no longer bear fruit, so the temple with its corruption would soon come to an end. Salvation would no longer be provided through the blood of animals, but through the ultimate sacrifice, once for all, of the Lamb of God. What a drama! What a bold exertion of Jesus' authority! What a powerful reminder that no longer would a person be redeemed by "the blood of goats and bulls . . ." but by "the blood of Christ who through the eternal Spirit offered himself without blemish to God . . ." (Hebrews 9:13–14).

The Fourth Assertion of Jesus' Authority: the Verbal Defense of His Claims (11:27—12:12)

Jesus not only portrayed his authority by dramatic actions, but he also verbally defended it in his teaching. The chief priests, scribes, and elders challenged him, asking (Mark 11:28), "By what authority are you doing these things?" Mark describes how Jesus, over the next few days, answered their question in a series of encounters, debates, and parables.

1. *Jesus answers the challenge to his authority (11:27–33).* There is a touch of ironic humor in the public exchange between Jesus and the leaders about authority. They thought they had Jesus in a corner. If Jesus answered that his authority was from God, they would charge Jesus with blasphemy. If Jesus said it was some kind of secular, human authority, they would charge Jesus with political insurrection. As Jesus often did, he answered their question with a question of his own. Jesus asked them (11:30), "'Was the baptism of John from heaven, or was it of human origin? Answer me.'"

> *If anyone doubts that Jesus claimed to be the Messiah, here is striking evidence that he did.*

With one subtle stroke, Jesus had put the leaders in rhetorical checkmate! If they admitted John's authority was from God, Jesus would say (11:31), "Why then did you not believe him?" If they said Jesus' authority was from men, the crowd to whom John was a hero would rise up against them. They were trapped. So, rather than conceding the debate, they falsely claimed (11:33), "We do not know." Their response was somewhat like taking the Fifth Amendment, "I refuse to answer on the grounds that it might tend to incriminate me."

2. *Jesus asserts his authority with a parable (12:1–12).* Here are the characters in the drama in the parable Jesus told:

The Owner and Provider of the Vineyard	God
The Vineyard Itself	Israel
The Tenants of the Vineyard	Leaders of Israel
The Servants of the Owner	The prophets, John the Baptist
The Son and Heir of the Owner	Jesus Christ

When we interpret parables like this one, we should not try to make each detail mean something. We should try to focus on the main lessons. So don't make too much of the hedge, the pit, the wine press, and the tower. The main idea is that the vineyard, Israel, was abundantly supplied by the Owner with all that was necessary for fruitful, happy service to God. The tenants failed to follow God's instructions, stubbornly rebuked God's messengers, and finally murdered God's Son. The judgment of the Owner fell on the tenants and the Son was vindicated.

The parable gives us a wonderful glimpse into the depths of God's heart. We learn that

(1) God is a loving and generous provider.
(2) God is willing to trust us with responsibilities in his kingdom.
(3) God is long-suffering, patient.
(4) God's patience has its limits.
(5) Ultimately God's justice will prevail.

Jesus' "Wrath"

These two incidents—the cursing of the tree and the "cleansing" of the temple (Mark 11:12–21) are very much alike. They are the only occasions where Jesus fiercely demonstrated what we might call righteous wrath. What lessons can be drawn from this? Consider:

- In the eyes of Jesus, are sins of omission (the fruitless tree) as serious as sins of commission (the desecration of the Temple)?
- Can we say that Jesus is just as displeased when we do nothing for the kingdom as he is when we sinfully violate its laws?
- Should we Christians define who we are by what we don't do or by what we do?

The parable also gives us a wonderful glimpse into the depth of Jesus' heart. We learn that

(1) Jesus saw himself not as another servant (prophet) but as God's only Son.
(2) Jesus knew he was going to die (another prophecy of Jesus' death).
(3) Jesus knew he would be resurrected and thus would ultimately triumph.

Too, the parable gives us a grim glimpse into the stubborn, rebellious hearts of sinful humanity.

David Garland of Baylor University compares this parable to the clever trap Nathan set for King David with his story of the ewe lamb (2 Samuel 12:1–15). After Nathan expressed his indignation at the actions of the rich owner, Nathan nailed David with this assertion (2 Sam. 12:7): "You are the man!" So Jesus trapped these hapless critics.[1] Like Nathan, as they listened to Jesus' story, they were probably nodding in agreement, rightly angry about the wicked and murderous tenants, until they realized, *He's talking about us! He's saying we are the vile, incorrigible, deadbeat tenants of God's vineyard!* Too late. Like David, "they realized that he had told this parable against them" (Mark 12:12).

> *Jesus not only portrayed his authority by dramatic actions, but he also verbally defended it in his teaching.*

3. *Jesus defends his authority against their traps (12:13–44).* Mark concludes this part of his gospel by recording the brilliant ability of Jesus to perceive and turn back the challenges of his critics. The trick question from the Pharisees about paying taxes to Caesar (12:13–17), the trick question from the Sadducees about the resurrection (12:18–27), and the trick question from the scribes about which is the greatest commandment (12:28–34)—all received stunning answers that parried their fierce thrusts.

The last four verses of chapter 12 tell how Jesus exerted his authority by watching and judging the stewardship of those who dropped their offering into the Temple treasury.

Conclusion

Some contemporary readers of the New Testament believe that it was the followers of Jesus who described him as the Messiah, the Son of God, and the Savior of the world, but that Jesus never made such claims himself. Those doubters need to study again with an open mind this convincing section of Mark's Gospel. There is no doubt that Mark's record shows Jesus boldly asserting his authority.

QUESTIONS

1. Does Jesus' critique of worship in the temple speak to worship in today's churches? How?

2. Do you think the descriptions of Jesus as "gentle and humble" (Matthew 11:29) and these descriptions of his righteous wrath are contradictory?

3. What are some of the ways contemporary doubters challenge the authority of Jesus?

4. What lessons can churches today learn from Jesus' parable of the tenants of the vineyard?

NOTES

1. David E. Garland, *Mark*, The NIV Application Commentary (Grand Rapids, Michigan: Zondervan Publishing House, 1996), 451.

Focal Text

Mark 13:1–37

Background

Mark 13:1–37

Main Idea

Jesus told his disciples to be alert and faithful to him in the way they lived and to beware of being led astray by people who claimed to know the future.

Question to Explore

How should we live in relation to the uncertainties of the future?

BONUS LESSON

Jesus Teaches About the Future

Study Aim

To summarize Jesus' teachings in Mark 13 and determine appropriate ways to be ready for the second coming of Christ

Study and Action Emphases

- Share the gospel of Jesus Christ with all people
- Equip people for ministry in the church and in the world

Quick Read

Jesus warned his troubled disciples about uncertain days ahead, advising them how to live with confidence in spite of an unknown future.

For the last few years, a series of novels about the end of the world has been on the best-seller list. One of the books has even been made into a movie. It's the first time this kind of literature has broken into the secular market with such success. While there has always been widespread curiosity about eschatology (the doctrine of last things), the popularity of these books suggests a heightened curiosity.

A similar curiosity about the future led four of Jesus' disciples to ask (Mark 13:4), "Tell us, when will this be, and what will be the sign that all these things are about to be accomplished?" Jesus' answer recorded in Mark 13 is one of the most difficult passages in Mark's Gospel—in the entire Bible for that matter. Jesus used ideas, terms, and symbols familiar to Jews in that day, but strange and unfamiliar to modern readers. Scholars call this chapter an example of "apocalyptic writing."

Especially popular during the 400 years between the Old and New Testaments, apocalyptic literature is a unique kind of writing unlike anything we know today. It employs dreams, visions, and Technicolor® word pictures to symbolize what will happen in the future, particularly during the last days before the end of the world. Apocalyptic writing is more like poetry than prose. It is an attempt to paint the unpaintable and speak the unspeakable. Such literature was never intended to be interpreted prosaically like a map of the future or a timetable of events to come. It should be read as visions not science, dreams not history.

Jesus chose the apparatus of apocalyptic language and imagery to answer the disciples' question about the future. They obviously understood that these broad strokes of picture language were intended to let them see a little of what God alone knows. If Jesus had wanted them to have a clear calendar of future events, he would have spelled out the details. Instead, Jesus gave them hope and encouragement as they faced uncertain times—in the near future (the destruction of the temple in Jerusalem) and in the more distant future (Jesus' second coming and the end of the world).

Wise interpreters, therefore, will read chapter thirteen in this light—not as a detailed roadmap or a specific timetable of events to satisfy our eschatological curiosity but as a source of hope enabling us to face the future with confidence. The chapter's value should not be lost in fruitless debates over millennial views. Instead, we should treasure its call to practical faith.

This chapter has been organized and outlined in dozens of ways. One helpful way is to tracc three strands of thought that are intertwined throughout Mark 13, as follows:

(1) The destruction of the Jerusalem and the temple
(2) The second coming of Jesus and the end of the world
(3) Admonitions to watch and be ready

The problem is to understand which verses relate to which strands. Apparently Mark was not inspired to

Mark 13:1–37

1 As he came out of the temple, one of his disciples said
to him, "Look, Teacher, what large stones and what large
buildings!" 2 Then Jesus asked him, "Do you see these
great buildings? Not one stone will be left here upon
another; all will be thrown down."

3 When he was sitting on the Mount of Olives opposite
the temple, Peter, James, John, and Andrew asked him
privately, 4 "Tell us, when will this be, and what will be
the sign that all these things are about to be accom-
plished?" 5 Then Jesus began to say to them, "Beware
that no one leads you astray. 6 Many will come in my
name and say, 'I am he!' and they will lead many astray.
7 When you hear of wars and rumors of wars, do not be
alarmed; this must take place, but the end is still to
come. 8 For nation will rise against nation, and kingdom
against kingdom; there will be earthquakes in various
places; there will be famines. This is but the beginning of
the birth pangs.

9 "As for yourselves, beware; for they will hand you over
to councils; and you will be beaten in synagogues; and
you will stand before governors and kings because of
me, as a testimony to them. 10 And the good news must
first be proclaimed to all nations. 11 When they bring you
to trial and hand you over, do not worry beforehand
about what you are to say; but say whatever is given you
at that time, for it is not you who speak, but the Holy
Spirit. 12 Brother will betray brother to death, and a father

his child, and children will rise against parents and have
them put to death; 13and you will be hated by all because
of my name. But the one who endures to the end will be
saved.

14"But when you see the desolating sacrilege set up
where it ought not to be (let the reader understand),
then those in Judea must flee to the mountains; 15the one
on the housetop must not go down or enter the house
to take anything away; 16the one in the field must not
turn back to get a coat. 17Woe to those who are pregnant
and to those who are nursing infants in those days! 18Pray
that it may not be in winter. 19For in those days there will
be suffering, such as has not been from the beginning of
the creation that God created until now, no, and never
will be. 20And if the Lord had not cut short those days, no
one would be saved; but for the sake of the elect, whom
he chose, he has cut short those days. 21And if anyone
says to you at that time, 'Look! Here is the Messiah!' or
'Look! There he is!'—do not believe it. 22False messiahs
and false prophets will appear and produce signs and
omens, to lead astray, if possible, the elect. 23But be alert;
I have already told you everything.

24"But in those days, after that suffering,
the sun will be darkened,
and the moon will not give its light,
25 and the stars will be falling from heaven,
and the powers in the heavens will be shaken.

26Then they will see 'the Son of Man coming in clouds'
with great power and glory. 27Then he will send out the

angels, and gather his elect from the four winds, from
the ends of the earth to the ends of heaven.
28"From the fig tree learn its lesson: as soon as its
branch becomes tender and puts forth its leaves, you
know that summer is near. 29So also, when you see these
things taking place, you know that he is near, at the very
gates. 30Truly I tell you, this generation will not pass away
until all these things have taken place. 31Heaven and
earth will pass away, but my words will not pass away.
32"But about that day or hour no one knows, neither
the angels in heaven, nor the Son, but only the Father.
33Beware, keep alert; for you do not know when the time
will come. 34It is like a man going on a journey, when he
leaves home and puts his slaves in charge, each with his
work, and commands the doorkeeper to be on the
watch. 35Therefore, keep awake—for you do not know
when the master of the house will come, in the evening,
or at midnight, or at cockcrow, or at dawn, 36or else he
may find you asleep when he comes suddenly. 37And
what I say to you I say to all: Keep awake."

give us a verbatim transcript of Jesus' discourse on Mount Olivet. Instead, Mark summarized it, perhaps not always putting it in what Western readers would call logical order. Furthermore, some scholars believe Mark collected other sayings of Jesus on this same subject and included some of them here as well. So, the following treatment is only one of several possible interpretations of this challenging passage.

Warnings Related to the Destruction of the Temple (13:1–23)

The incident in chapter thirteen took place during the last week of our Lord's earthly ministry. It was thirty or more years later, about AD 65, when Mark wrote about the incident. Mark's Gospel was intended primarily for believers in Rome who were having to deal with the persecutions of Nero. Other readers in Jerusalem were facing the turmoil of Roman occupation and rebellions that would come to a head in AD 70 when Emperor Titus besieged and destroyed the city. Our interpretation should begin with what this chapter must have meant to those first readers.

The chapter's value should not be lost in fruitless debates over millennial views. Instead, we should treasure its call to practical faith.

13:1–2. For the final time, Jesus left the temple. Crossing the Kidron Valley with his disciples, Jesus sat down to teach them. Herod's temple must have been a dazzling sight, dominating the city skyline, its gold decorations reflecting the sun. (See the brief article, "The Three Temples," for a history of its construction.) As the disciples walked away from the temple, they were sure it would stand until the end of time. What a shock, then, to hear Jesus predict its total destruction.

13:3–4. More than likely, all the disciples were with Jesus, but the four who had been with Jesus the longest—Peter, Andrew, James, and John—pulled him aside in an attempt to get some privileged information about the future.

13:5–13. As the disciples sat down in customary teaching/learning fashion, the formal discourse began ("Jesus began to say to them . . . ."). What a dramatic backdrop for Jesus' lesson. Mount Moriah, on which the temple was built, stood 2470 feet above sea level. To the east, across the Kidron Valley, the Mount of Olives stood 200 feet higher than the temple hill.

Sometimes the Holy Spirit inspired biblical writers to use a variety of literary devices—poetry, parables, acrostics, etc. Here, Mark employed a literary device called a *chiasmus*, a rhetorical technique that inverts the second of two parallel phrases. The pattern is *A B C*, then *C B A*. For example:

A. Deceivers (13:5–6) "Beware"
  B. International Wars (13:7–8) "When you hear . . . "
    C. Persecution of Christians (13: 9–13) "Beware"
  B́. War in Judea (13:14–20) "When you see . . . "
Á. Deceivers (13:21–23) "Look"

Since the disciples were facing an unpredictable future, Jesus gave these warnings:

(1) False teachers, exploiting dark times, would take advantage of their anxiety and seek to lead them astray (13:5–6). Jesus repeated similar warnings in 13:21–23.
(2) There would be wars and natural disasters, but these are inevitable elements of sinful existence,

The Three Temples

The first temple, built by Solomon, was completed about 950 BC. The Babylonians destroyed it in 587 BC.

Zerubbabel rebuilt the temple on the same site as Solomon's, finally completing it in 515 BC. It was not very grand, but Zerubbabel's temple was used for 500 years. Zerubbabel's temple is known as the second temple.

During the time between the Old Testament and the New Testament, a Greek ruler, Antiochus Epiphanes, desecrated this second temple. In 168 BC he sacrificed a swine on the sacred altar, brought images of Zeus into the Holy of Holies, and turned rooms of the temple into brothels.

On this same site, Herod later built the third temple, a magnificent structure beyond anything ever built in Jerusalem. About 19 BC, after eighteen months, the main temple was finished. However, the entire complex around the temple itself was continually being expanded and eventually included about one-sixth of the total area of Jerusalem, about thirty-five acres. It was still under construction when the disciples said to Jesus, "Look, Teacher, what large stones and what large buildings!" (Mk. 13:1) When the Romans destroyed it in AD 70, the temple was still unfinished.

---

not signs of the end (13:7–8). "This must take place, but the end is still to come" (13:7). Such calamities will occur before the end, but they do not predict it.

(3) The disciples would face persecution, similar to what Jesus faced (13:9–13). Just as Jesus was handed over to councils; tried before governors and kings; and beaten, hated, and betrayed by associates, so the disciples would be persecuted. Jesus encouraged them with the promise that the Holy Spirit would be with them to see them through. Years later, the experiences of Paul before synagogues, governors like Festus and Felix, and kings like Agrippa graphically fulfilled this prediction.

Apparently this subject brought to mind the need to spread the gospel to all nations, even in the midst of persecution. Thus Jesus declared that evangelism is a divine necessity. One irony of history is that Christianity has often spread and grown because of persecution. Fleeing Christians became missionaries; martyrs inspired and encouraged others. This led George Bernard Shaw to conclude that the best way to stimulate the Christian faith was to feed as many believers as possible to the lions!

As the disciples walked away from the temple, they were sure it would stand until the end of time. What a shock, then, to hear Jesus predict its total destruction.

13:14–23. Having described certain coming events that are not necessarily signs but that are expected in every age, Jesus then gave the disciples a specific indicator of the future destruction of Jerusalem. When the disciples saw "the desolating sacrilege set up

Evening Worship
6:00 p.m.

Hymn 428	Victory In Jesus
Prayer	
Welcome and Announcements	
Hymns 361	We Have Come into His House
379	Brethren, We Have Met to Worship
448	Just A Closer Walk With Thee
Offering	
Special Music	Daisy Roberts
Message	Bro. Joe
Invitation 321	The Savior is Waiting
Benediction	When We All Get to Heaven

Churchwide
FELLOWSHIP TONIGHT
Following p.m. Service
In honor of
Derek & Sara Brian

This Morning we will vote by ballot to make Dean Cornelius our permanent Music Director.

BAPTIST MEN'S MEETING
Today, 4:00 P.M.

VBS

July 8-12

See Wendy if you would like
to help in some area

Our first VBS planning meeting
will be today
at 5:00 p.m.
Anyone that has signed up,
or wants to help in any way,
is invited to attend.
This is a great chance for
outreach for our church
and we need all the help
we can get.
Hope to see you there!

THANK YOU!

I want to thank each of you at Wildwood Baptist Church for your prayers, the blessings of God for the weekend revival and for the love offering.

Bro. Chuck Dooley

Be of good cheer;
It is I;
Be not afraid
Matthew 14:27

WILDWOOD BAPTIST CHURCH

531 So. Walker — Mesquite, TX

972-285-8201

Joe McCammon , Pastor

Morning Worship - June 2, 2002

Opportunities for the week
Call to Worship People Of God Choir
Hymn
Scripture and Prayer Derek Brian
Meet, Greet and Move Your Feet
Welcome to our guests Bro. Joe
Fellowship Chorus In the Family of God Choir
Children's Choir
Children's Sermon Bro. Joe
Praise Medley Holy, this place is Holy,
Come now and feast on His word.
Holy, this place is Holy,
For this is the house of the Lord. Repeat
*__This is Holy Ground__, we're standing on Holy Ground
For the Lord is here, and where He is, is Holy.*Repeat
We are standing on Holy Ground.
And I know that there are angels all around
Let us praise Jesus now.
We are standing in His presence on Holy Ground.
Offertory Hymn 10 How Great Thou Art
Tithes & Offerings
Choral Message in Song It Will Be Worth It All
Message Bro. Joe
Invitation 300 Without Him
Benediction How Great Thou Art

where it ought not to be," they should flee from the city to the safety of the mountains, because the destruction would be imminent. This term, "desolating sacrilege," sometimes translated "the abomination of desolation" (KJV), comes from Daniel 9:27; 11:31; 12:11. Does the term refer to a person, a thing, or an occurrence? The language would allow any of these possibilities. It probably refers to some pagan pollution of the temple such as the abominable sacrilege of Antiochus Epiphanes in 168 BC, when he led in desecrating the temple.

Our interpretation should begin with what this chapter must have meant to those first readers.

Whatever it was, it would have been recognizable to the first readers, and it would be their signal to flee to the mountains, because the tribulation would be unimaginable (13:19). Pregnant and nursing women would have trouble moving quickly enough, and bad weather would make flight hard. But the good news was, there would be time to get away—not enough time to get things from the house downstairs or to pick up a coat, but time nevertheless. (This obviously doesn't refer to the end of the world, for there would be no need to flee to mountains or worry about winter!)

Jesus' prophecy came true. When the Jewish rebellion against Rome broke out in AD 66, the soldiers of the Roman Empire besieged Jerusalem and eventually destroyed it. The war ended when the fortress at Masada fell in AD 73. According to the Jewish historian,

Tim and Ethyl

Tim and Ethyl were both considered expert Bible teachers in the church, but they took two different positions on the subject of the second coming of Jesus

Ethyl was preoccupied with the subject, exploring different millennial views, making charts of end-time prophecies, specializing on the Books of Daniel and Revelation. To her, the doctrine of the second coming was the most important in the Bible.

Tim, on the other hand, was turned off by what he called "fanatical speculation" about the end of the world, and Tim never dealt with the subject in his teaching.

How would you evaluate each of these approaches?

Josephus, more than one million people died in the Jerusalem siege, and 100,000 were taken captive. The temple was completely destroyed. Only a few of the foundation stones that make up the present wailing wall remained. Eusebius, writing in AD 325, reported that some Christians in Jerusalem remembered Jesus' advice and fled across the Jordan to the mountain city of Pella in Decapolis.

The unusual parenthetical phrase in 13:14, "let the reader understand," was an instruction from Mark to the one who would publicly read the gospel to the churches. The people of that day had no individual Bibles, and so public reading was customary. It was probably intended to alert the reader to an irregular grammatical construction. The noun translated "sacrilege" is neuter, and the participle translated "set up" or "standing" (NASB, NIV, KJV) is masculine. Mark was telling the reader not to correct the irregularity. He meant it like it was written to suggest that the sacrilege refers to a person. This would be similar to our method of placing "sic" after an intentionally misspelled word. Thus Mark was saying something like this: *When you see that thing, the desolating sacrilege standing where he (sic) ought not to be. . . .*"

Perhaps the clearest verse in the entire chapter is 13:32, "But about that day or hour no one knows, neither the angels in heaven, nor the Son, but only the Father."

This section on the destruction of Jerusalem concludes as it began, with a warning about deceivers (13:21–22).

Warnings Related to the Second Coming and the End of the World (13:24–27)

In answering the disciples' question, Jesus went far beyond the events related to the destruction of the temple. When Jesus said, "In those days, after that suffering" (that is, after the suffering in Jerusalem described in 13:19), Jesus was pointing to the distant time when he would return. How long after the suffering in Jerusalem would this occur? Jesus did not say. Rather, with a deliberate ambiguity about time, Jesus drew aside the curtain a little and let us see certain events that would occur at the time of Jesus' return.

. . . If Jesus is uncertain of God's timing, shouldn't we be suspicious of anyone who claims to be able to predict the date?

Jesus indicated that the end would come suddenly, without much warning. Jesus used apocalyptic language from the prophets to describe a massive disruption in the natural order. The sun, moon, and stars would be darkened by a cosmic power failure! Then Jesus would come in power and glory.

Nothing is said here about the judgment, resurrection, heaven, or hell. These verses say only that when the Son of Man comes, he will gather from the four winds "his elect," that is, his people, people who have faithfully responded to the gospel.

One irony of history is that Christianity has often spread and grown because of persecution.

Jesus refused to grant the disciples' request for a timetable, but these two things are clear:

(1) The end of the temple must happen before the end of time, but (2) the end of the temple does not denote the end. What might lie between the two events is left unsaid. To be sure, the first-century believers expected Jesus' return in their lifetime. This passage seems to teach that such an expectation of Jesus' imminent return is the appropriate position for every generation.

Warnings Related to the Need for Watchfulness (13:28–37)

13:28–31. Jesus concluded the Olivet Discourse with two parables. The first is about a fig tree and relates to the destruction of Jerusalem. Just as the sprouting of leaves on a fig tree signal the sure coming of summer, so the signs Jesus had given the disciples were a sure warning of the destruction of Jerusalem. Jesus told them it was "near, at the very gates . . . this generation will not pass away before all these things take place" (13:29–30). Sure enough, within forty years (AD 70), the temple and the city were in ruins.

13:32–37. The second parable relates to Jesus' second coming. Jesus is like the master of the house returning from a journey. He has put his servants in charge, but they do not know when he will return. The servants must constantly keep watch so they will not be surprised. So Jesus' followers, not knowing the time of his coming, must be constantly on watch.

Perhaps the clearest verse in the entire chapter is 13:32, "But about that day or hour no one knows, neither the angels in heaven, nor the Son, but only the Father." The Lord is surely coming again, but no one knows when—including Jesus. Jesus was content to leave this unquestioningly in the hand of God. Jesus apparently limited himself when he took on human form. So if Jesus is uncertain of God's timing, shouldn't we be suspicious of anyone who claims to be able to predict the date?

The Main Point

The story is told of Tolstoy, the renowned Russian writer, who was working in his garden when a man approached him and asked, "What would you do if you suddenly learned you had but one day to live?" Tolstoy replied, "I would continue working in my garden."

The good news is that the future is secure in Jesus Christ.

The main point of this passage is that believers should live faithfully in the present time, expecting Jesus to return at any moment, as he promised. They are to watch, be ready, preach the gospel to the whole world, and depend on the Holy Spirit to guide them. They should not be surprised or caught off guard. If believers live in this manner, they will not need to run around getting things straight before the last day.

So this difficult passage:

- Warns us about religious phonies who exploit dark times and lead believers astray
- Promises the Holy Spirit will sustain us in the inevitable persecution we will face
- Challenges us to get on with the main task—proclaiming the gospel
- Reminds us that no one but God knows when the end time will arrive

The disciples to whom Jesus spoke these words were worried about the future. In AD 65, the first readers of this gospel were concerned about their future. And now, we twenty-first century readers are concerned about the future, too. The good news is that the future is secure in Jesus Christ.

QUESTIONS

1. Can you name some "false messiahs" in recent years that seem to fit the danger Jesus warned about in Mark 13:5–6, 21–23? (For example, Jim Jones)

2. Why do you suppose Jesus chose not to give us exact dates related to Jesus' second coming and the end of the world?

3. There is much about this chapter that is difficult to understand, but what things in this chapter are absolutely clear?

4. Is it right to expect the return of Jesus at any time?

Focal Text

Mark 14:12–26, 32–42

Background

Mark 14:1–42

Main Idea

Jesus willingly gave his life in faithfulness to his God-given mission.

Question to Explore

What is worth a person's life?

LESSON ELEVEN

Jesus Gives His Life

Study Aim

To identify ways I will express gratitude for Jesus' giving his life

Study and Action Emphases

- Share the gospel of Jesus Christ with all people
- Equip people for ministry in the church and in the world
- Develop Christian families

Quick Read

Aware of his impending crucifixion, Jesus created a "supper" to help his followers remember his death. Then, in Gethsemane, Jesus prayed a prayer of surrendering to his Father's will.

A Hollywood film pictures a suspenseful moment when four climbers are ascending Mount Everest. They are tied to a safety rope, so that if one falls, the others can anchor their picks and cleats in the ice and pull the fallen climber to safety. Suddenly, the lowest climber slips and is suspended in air by the safety rope. Surprised and with no time to react, the next two climbers one by one are pulled down as well, until only the highest climber is anchored to the mountain. The lead climber and the tethered rope can hold two of the fallen mountaineers, but not three. Realizing the situation, the lowest climber who slipped pulls out his knife and cuts the rope above his head, falling to his death so his comrades can be saved.

Such examples of self-sacrifice for others remind us of Romans 5:7, "Rarely will anyone die for a righteous person—though perhaps for a good person someone might actually dare to die." However, this lesson tells us that our Lord willingly "cut the rope" to save—not righteous or good people—but sinners like you and me. "While we were yet sinners, Christ died for us" (Rom. 5:8, NASB). Nowhere in the records of self-sacrifice is there a more powerful account of one person giving his life that others might live.

Jesus Creates a Living Memorial of His Death (14:12–26)

The Passover, celebrating the "passing over" of the Israelites when the Egyptian firstborn were slain,

Mark 14:12–26, 32–42

12 On the first day of Unleavened Bread, when the
Passover lamb is sacrificed, his disciples said to him,
"Where do you want us to go and make the preparations
for you to eat the Passover?" 13 So he sent two of his disci-
ples, saying to them, "Go into the city, and a man carry-
ing a jar of water will meet you; follow him, 14 and
wherever he enters, say to the owner of the house, 'The
Teacher asks, Where is my guest room where I may eat
the Passover with my disciples?' 15 He will show you a
large room upstairs, furnished and ready. Make prepara-
tions for us there." 16 So the disciples set out and went to
the city, and found everything as he had told them; and
they prepared the Passover meal.

17 When it was evening, he came with the twelve. 18 And
when they had taken their places and were eating, Jesus
said, "Truly I tell you, one of you will betray me, one who
is eating with me." 19 They began to be distressed and to
say to him one after another, "Surely, not I?" 20 He said to
them, "It is one of the twelve, one who is dipping bread
into the bowl with me. 21 For the Son of Man goes as it is
written of him, but woe to that one by whom the Son of
Man is betrayed! It would have been better for that one
not to have been born."

22 While they were eating, he took a loaf of bread, and
after blessing it he broke it, gave it to them, and said,
"Take; this is my body." 23 Then he took a cup, and after
giving thanks he gave it to them, and all of them drank
from it. 24 He said to them, "This is my blood of the

covenant, which is poured out for many. 25Truly I tell you,
I will never again drink of the fruit of the vine until that
day when I drink it new in the kingdom of God."
26When they had sung the hymn, they went out to the
Mount of Olives.

32They went to a place called Gethsemane; and he said
to his disciples, "Sit here while I pray." 33He took with him
Peter and James and John, and began to be distressed
and agitated. 34And he said to them, "I am deeply
grieved, even to death; remain here, and keep awake."
35And going a little farther, he threw himself on the
ground and prayed that, if it were possible, the hour
might pass from him. 36He said, "Abba, Father, for you all
things are possible; remove this cup from me; yet, not
what I want, but what you want." 37He came and found
them sleeping; and he said to Peter, "Simon, are you
asleep? Could you not keep awake one hour? 38Keep
awake and pray that you may not come into the time of
trial; the spirit indeed is willing, but the flesh is weak."
39And again he went away and prayed, saying the same
words. 40And once more he came and found them sleep-
ing, for their eyes were very heavy; and they did not
know what to say to him. 41He came a third time and said
to them, "Are you still sleeping and taking your rest?
Enough! The hour has come; the Son of Man is betrayed
into the hands of sinners. 42Get up, let us be going. See,
my betrayer is at hand."

was a meal eaten on the evening of the15th of the Jewish month Nisan, March/April of modern calendars. Merged with the Passover celebration, the Feast of Unleavened Bread was a celebration of the barley harvest and a reminder of the time when the children of Israel ate unleavened bread while leaving Egypt.

Each head of household brought a lamb to the temple on the afternoon of the 14th of Nisan. The priests would slaughter the animal, sprinkle the blood on the altar, and burn the fat and entrails on the altar. Then the priests would return the carcass to the worshipper. The carcass was to be cooked somewhere within the city limits and eaten indoors that evening.

Nowhere in the records of self-sacrifice is there a more powerful account of one person giving his life that others might live.

Many pilgrims flocked into Jerusalem during this Passover and Unleavened Bread festival. Supposedly, every Jewish male within fifteen miles of Jerusalem was to attend the festival, but since every Jewish man wanted to eat the Passover at least once in Jerusalem before he died, far more than that came. Estimates run from 250,000 to 3,000,000. Josephus, the Jewish historian, tells how Cestius the Palestinian governor asked the high priest to take a census of lambs slain in one annual Passover Feast in Jerusalem. The number according to Josephus was 256,500. Estimating ten people to one lamb, there may have been more than 2.5 million worshippers that year.[1]

Riots and rebellions frequently occurred during this festival. Therefore, the Roman governors found it necessary to move temporarily to Jerusalem from headquarters in Caesarea so they could better monitor the situation and maintain order.

1. *Preparing the Passover meal (14:12–16).* Since Jesus and the disciples were in Bethany, they had to go to Jerusalem to purchase the necessary items, bake the unleavened bread, prepare the sauce with bitter herbs, have the lamb slain at the temple, and roast it.

A Passover Meal?

Here Mark says that the meal Jesus and his disciples shared was eaten on the day the lambs were sacrificed (Mark 14:12). John's Gospel, however, states that Jesus and his disciples observed the Last Supper the night before the Passover (John 13:1, 29). Passover was the day the lambs were sacrificed. This problem has led some to question whether the meal in Mark 14 could be a true Passover meal. There is some help in remembering the large numbers of worshippers who were in Jerusalem trying to kill and eat the Passover at the same time. With such crowds, the Jewish leaders apparently gave some latitude as to the exact date the meal was eaten. Possibly the disciples observed the meal a day earlier than the actual Passover. One thing seems clear; the meal Jesus and his disciples shared had every appearance of a Passover meal.[6]

So Jesus sent two of them (Peter and John, according to Luke 22:8) with cryptic instructions to follow "a man carrying a jar of water" to an upper room where they would celebrate the Passover (Mark 14:13).

Jesus used the coded signal and the secret instructions to prevent his premature arrest. Knowing when the man would be passing by with the waterpot is another indication of his supernatural knowledge. Since transporting water was typically a woman's job, such a man would be easy to spot. One wonders about the identity of this secret Jerusalem disciple. He carried a water jar, but his name is not known.

> *Jesus made it clear that he is the true Passover Lamb whose shed and sprinkled blood establishes a new relationship with God.*

Most houses in Jerusalem had one to four rooms on one level. So an upper room probably indicated a wealthier home. "Furnished" (14:15) here probably means the room had a couch, carpet, and vessels. Today travelers to Jerusalem are shown a room that is supposed to be the place, but it is of much later construction, probably about AD 1100. While traditions going back to the fourth century identify this location, the building itself would probably not have survived the destruction of the city in AD 70.

The entire account shows Jesus in control, directing the entire drama of his death. He is not a helpless victim or martyr. But as the Lord of all circumstances, Jesus is free, in control, arranging all the events, giving himself up freely to the cross. Nothing could drag Jesus there but his own love.

2. *Eating the Passover meal (14: 17–21).* The disciples probably reclined in a circle around a low table, leaning on their left elbows and eating with their right hands. Serving as the host, Jesus began the observance with a grave announcement of his betrayal. "One of you will betray me, one who is eating with me" (14:18). In ancient times, eating together was an act of friendship. The most despicable act was betraying a friend shortly after sharing a meal. No wonder the disciples respond in shock. Their question literally expected a negative answer (14:19), "Surely not I?"

The entire account shows Jesus in control, directing the entire drama of his death.

Very likely, Jesus and the disciples followed the typical procedure for a Passover meal.[2] The host would give thanks. Then the group would share the first cup and eat the lamb, the unleavened bread, and bitter herbs. After this, the host would ask why this night was different. The answer from the participants was to recite the story of Exodus. They would then sing the first part of the *Hallel*, Psalm 113 (or 113—114), and share the second cup. Next, the host would give thanks. They would drink the third cup and resume eating. The ceremony would conclude before midnight with the singing of the second part of the *Hallel* (Psalms 115—18 or 114—118) and the sharing of the fourth cup. Jesus apparently waited until after all this was completed before instituting his special memorial meal.

3. *Inaugurating a new memorial meal (14:22–26).* After the Passover, Jesus took some broken bread and a cup, then "blessing" it (14:22). Jesus used a common piece of bread so that every time Jesus' followers sat down for a meal, they would think of this night and his death on the cross for them. The new memorial is a multi-media reminder involving all our senses: sight, touch, taste, smell, and hearing. It has been observed somewhere around the world every Lord's day since.

In Mark 14:24, Jesus identified the new memorial meal with a new covenant. Just as the blood of an animal sacrifice sealed the covenant God made with Israel at Sinai, so now the blood of Jesus would seal the new covenant God was making with God's new people, the church. Jesus made it clear that he is the true Passover Lamb whose shed and sprinkled blood establishes a new relationship with God. Anyone who denies that Jesus taught the sacrificial character and atoning power of his death needs to read this passage again. Jesus said plainly, "This is my blood . . . which is poured out for many" (14:24).

Since Mark uses the term "fruit of the vine" (14:25) instead of wine, some have suggested that Jesus used unfermented grape juice. While unfermented wine was sometimes used in ancient times, the wine used in the Passover would be fermented. However, according to some New Testament scholars, wine in biblical days was usually diluted with water and thus had less alcoholic content than wine today.[3]

Most of the meal was eaten in a spirit of gloom, but Jesus ended the gathering with a note of hope, pointing to the "day when I drink it new in the kingdom of God" (14:25). Even in the face of betrayal and death, Jesus expressed confidence that ultimately he would be vindicated by God's reign. With that hope ringing in their ears, the disciples sang a hymn (probably Psalm 118) and left the upper room. What deep impressions of that night must have remained with Simon Peter, who later told this story to Mark.

Jesus trusted his Father's love as a little child trusts the love of the best earthly father.

Jesus Prays to the Father with Suffering and Surrender (14:32–42)

Reading this passage, we feel we are treading on holy ground. Obviously, Jesus intended that we see him struggle, because he invited Peter, James, and John to witness what happened. But we get the impression that our gaze at this holy scene should be restrained, reverent. We are not to stare too closely or analyze too logically. Rather, we are to watch humbly, from a distance.

Luke located Gethsemane (meaning *oil-press*) on the Mount of Olives, indicating it was a familiar retreat. John called it a garden (John 18:1). The exact site is unknown. In fact, visitors to Jerusalem today will be shown one site by the Latin church, another by the Armenians, another by the Greek Orthodox church, and still another by the Russian Orthodox church.

Since pilgrims in Jerusalem for the Passover frequently spent the night outdoors, the disciples probably assumed they were going to camp there under the stars. This might explain why they fell asleep so readily. Jesus knew the night would be cut short by his arrest and trial. Jesus went there to be encouraged by fellowship with those who loved him and primarily to pray to his Father.

Ironically, Jesus invited Peter, James, and John to follow him closer into Gethsemane. Think of it:

- Peter, whose brassy boast was, "Even though they all become deserters, I will not. . . . Even though I must die with you, I will not deny you" (Mark 14:29, 31)
- James and John, who boldly promised they could drink Jesus' cup and endure Jesus' baptism (Mark 10:39)

Jesus now gave them an opportunity to prove their claims. They failed miserably.

Jesus' Gethsemane prayer shows us three important truths.

1. *Jesus was aware of his Father's love (14:36).* Jesus said, "Abba, Father, for you all things are possible"

(14:36). It is sometimes said that Jesus was the first to call God "Father," but actually, centuries before Jesus came, the Jews used the term "Father" to address God.[4] However, Jews would never have used the familiar, intimate term "Abba," which is similar to our English word *daddy*. In using this term, Jesus revealed that he held a special, close relationship with God. Jesus also acknowledged God's omnipotence, "For you all things are possible" (14:36). Jesus trusted his Father's love as a little child trusts the love of the best earthly father.

Jesus obviously believed prayer made a difference.

2. *Jesus did not want to suffer and die (14:36).* Jesus prayed, "Remove this cup from me" (14:36). The gospels don't often show us the human emotions of Jesus, but here those emotions are described in graphic, almost shocking, directness. He was "distressed and agitated" (14:33). He was crushed by a sense of loneliness, by the feeling that he was not only being betrayed but also deserted. This time, Jesus didn't hear the Father's voice from heaven saying, "You are my Son, the Beloved" (1:14). There was no dove descending and lighting upon Jesus to encourage him. No angels came to minister to Jesus. Even Jesus' closest friends let him down, dozing a few feet away. Jesus poured out his soul in heart-rending anguish all alone.

In his humanity, Jesus didn't want to die. He was thirty-three years old. No one wants to die so young.

"My Body . . . My Blood"

For centuries, Christians have disagreed over the meaning of the words, "This is my body . . . this is my blood" (Mark 14:22, 24). The Roman Catholic tradition considers the meaning to be literal. In that view, the bread and cup are really, actually, the body and blood of Jesus. How would you explain the Baptist position that these words of Jesus are figurative? Here is a checklist of reasons:

1. The Aramaic spoken by Jesus did not use the word *is*. The Aramaic literally says, *This—my body . . . this—my blood.*
2. Jesus was physically present when he spoke the words, thus seeming to rule out a literal interpretation of the bread being his body.
3. The context of Jesus' words is the Passover ceremony, which was rich with symbolism, making it natural for Jesus' words to be symbolic as well.
4. The literal drinking of blood was offensive to the Jews, even forbidden by Scripture (Leviticus 7:26)

Jesus really did fear death, instinctively recoiling from it. Jesus knew what crucifixion involved, and he shuddered to think of it. Later, when some of Jesus' followers were called upon to die for him, it must have been reassuring to remember that their Savior faced the fear of death too. Jesus understood what they were feeling, and he would see them through. After all, the cross would lose all its value if it had been easy for Jesus!

In Mark's account we also see something more sacred than mere human trembling at the thought of death. Jesus was also feeling the crush of the sins of the whole world. When Jesus bore our sins, he suffered not only physically but also psychologically.

We find encouragement for us in Jesus' emotional plea to the Father. Jesus obviously believed prayer made a difference. He believed that God listens and grants our requests according to God's overall providence. When we're in distress, we don't have to worry about grammar, proper style, posture, or politeness in our prayer. We too can cry out to God without hesitation, confident that God will hear us.

3. *In spite of Jesus' anguish, Jesus submitted absolutely to his Father's will (14:36).* Jesus prayed, "Not what I want but what you want" (14:36). Thirty years earlier, Jesus' mother Mary had prayed a similar prayer. When God chose her to bear God's only Son, Mary, afraid and troubled, responded with a beautiful prayer of submission, "Here am I, the servant of the Lord; let it be with me according to your word" (Luke 1:38). Surely growing up in a home where his mother prayed, "Let it be with me according to your word," must have made it easier for Jesus to pray, "Not what I want, but what you want."

Years later, looking back on this night, Peter and the others must have had deep regrets.

After such a moving prayer, we're shocked to read how the disciples let Jesus down. Instead of watching out for Jesus and praying with him, they dozed off. Just as Simon Peter would later deny Jesus three times, so now he fell asleep three times. Years later, looking back on this night, Peter and the others must have had deep regrets. How ashamed they must have been at their faithlessness, how sorry for what they had missed, how regretful for the opportunity they had lost.

Let us be faithful to our Lord.

Note that a nameless woman anointed Jesus for his burial while his disciples rebuked her, a bystander carried Jesus' cross when his followers ran way in fear, and a pagan centurion confessed that Jesus was the Son of God while his witnesses were silent. A Sanhedrin member obtained Jesus' body and buried it in his own tomb. Women followers stood by Jesus at Calvary and later went to anoint the body, but male disciples betrayed Jesus and fled for their lives. Peter, James, and John did not keep watch. Rather they fell asleep.[5] Let us be faithful to our Lord.

QUESTIONS

1. Do you think the man with the water jar was a signal Jesus had pre-arranged, or do you think the incident was an evidence of Jesus' foreknowledge that the man would be in Jerusalem at the proper time?

2. Why did Jesus choose the Passover feast as the time to establish the memorial meal we now call the Lord's Supper?

3. Why did Jesus feel it necessary to establish a reminder that he died as a sacrifice for the sins of the world?

4. How does Jesus' agonizing prayer in the Garden of Gethsemane illustrate his divine-human nature?

5. What does Jesus' giving of himself say to you about how you should respond?

NOTES

1. William Barclay, *The Gospel of Mark,* The Daily Study Bible (Philadelphia: The Westminster Press, 1956), 340.
2. James A. Brooks, *Mark*, The New American Commentary, vol. 23 (Nashville: Broadman Press, 1991), 228.
3. Brooks, 229.
4. David E. Garland, *Mark*, The NIV Application Commentary (Grand Rapids, Michigan: Zondervan Publishing House, 1996), 540.
5. Garland, 543.
6. Brooks, 224–226.

Focal Text

Mark 14:53—15:20

Background

Mark 14:43—15:20

Main Idea

In contrast to the other people involved in his trial, Jesus responded with calm and conviction.

Question to Explore

How do you respond to challenges to your faith?

LESSON TWELVE

Jesus Is Condemned

Study Aim

To contrast how Jesus responded to the events of his trial with how the other people involved responded

Study and Action Emphases

- Share the gospel of Jesus Christ with all people
- Equip people for ministry in the church and in the world

Quick Read

During the last hours before Jesus' death, Jesus faced every challenge with calm confidence in his Father's care. Jesus' demeanor contrasted sharply with the response of others around him.

In 1805, Sir Francis Beaufort devised a scale of wind force still used by weather forecasters today. It ranks the wind from "light air" (1–3 mph) to "hurricane" (73–136 mph). Any wind from 0 to 1 mph is described as "calm." "Calm" also describes human behavior that is unruffled and serene. Mark Twain spoke of "the calm confidence of a Christian with four aces," suggesting it's easy to be calm when everything's going right. It takes real courage, however, to be confident and tranquil in the midst of crises.

The calm self-control of Jesus during the last hours before the cross stands in sharp contrast to the frantic, turbulent behavior of those around him. One way to study this passage is to compare the calmness of Jesus with the conduct of Judas, the High Priest, Simon Peter, the Sanhedrin mob, Pilate, and the Roman soldiers.

Judas Iscariot (14:43–52)

One day about 4 BC, in the village of Kerioth, a baby boy was born. His father and mother, grateful for his birth and anticipating the promise of his manhood, named him *Praise*. Friends and family brought gifts to celebrate the birth.

At about the same time, in the village of Bethlehem, a baby boy was born. His father and mother, grateful for his birth and fully aware of the promise of

Mark 14:53–72

53They took Jesus to the high priest; and all the chief
priests, the elders, and the scribes were assembled.
54Peter had followed him at a distance, right into the
courtyard of the high priest; and he was sitting with the
guards, warming himself at the fire. 55Now the chief
priests and the whole council were looking for testimony
against Jesus to put him to death; but they found none.
56For many gave false testimony against him, and their
testimony did not agree. 57Some stood up and gave false
testimony against him, saying, 58"We heard him say, 'I
will destroy this temple that is made with hands, and in
three days I will build another, not made with hands.'"
59But even on this point their testimony did not agree.
60Then the high priest stood up before them and asked
Jesus, "Have you no answer? What is it that they testify
against you?" 61But he was silent and did not answer.
Again the high priest asked him, "Are you the Messiah,
the Son of the Blessed One?" 62Jesus said, "I am; and

> 'you will see the Son of Man
> seated at the right hand of the Power,'
> and 'coming with the clouds of heaven.'"

63Then the high priest tore his clothes and said, "Why do
we still need witnesses? 64You have heard his blasphemy!
What is your decision?" All of them condemned him as
deserving death. 65Some began to spit on him, to blind-
fold him, and to strike him, saying to him, "Prophesy!"
The guards also took him over and beat him.

66While Peter was below in the courtyard, one of the servant-girls of the high priest came by. 67When she saw Peter warming himself, she stared at him and said, "You also were with Jesus, the man from Nazareth." 68But he denied it, saying, "I do not know or understand what you are talking about." And he went out into the forecourt. Then the cock crowed. 69And the servant-girl, on seeing him, began again to say to the bystanders, "This man is one of them." 70But again he denied it. Then after a little while the bystanders again said to Peter, "Certainly you are one of them; for you are a Galilean." 71But he began to curse, and he swore an oath, "I do not know this man you are talking about." 72At that moment the cock crowed for the second time. Then Peter remembered that Jesus had said to him, "Before the cock crows twice, you will deny me three times." And he broke down and wept.

Mark 15:1–20

1As soon as it was morning, the chief priests held a consultation with the elders and scribes and the whole council. They bound Jesus, led him away, and handed him over to Pilate. 2Pilate asked him, "Are you the King of the Jews?" He answered him, "You say so." 3Then the chief priests accused him of many things. 4Pilate asked him again, "Have you no answer? See how many charges they bring against you." 5But Jesus made no further reply, so that Pilate was amazed.

[6]Now at the festival he used to release a prisoner for
them, anyone for whom they asked. [7]Now a man called
Barabbas was in prison with the rebels who had commit-
ted murder during the insurrection. [8]So the crowd came
and began to ask Pilate to do for them according to his
custom. [9]Then he answered them, "Do you want me to
release for you the King of the Jews?" [10]For he realized
that it was out of jealousy that the chief priests had
handed him over. [11]But the chief priests stirred up the
crowd to have him release Barabbas for them instead.
[12]Pilate spoke to them again, "Then what do you wish me
to do with the man you call the King of the Jews?" [13]They
shouted back, "Crucify him!" [14]Pilate asked them, "Why,
what evil has he done?" But they shouted all the more,
"Crucify him!" [15]So Pilate, wishing to satisfy the crowd,
released Barabbas for them; and after flogging Jesus, he
handed him over to be crucified.

[16]Then the soldiers led him into the courtyard of the
palace (that is, the governor's headquarters); and they
called together the whole cohort. [17]And they clothed him
in a purple cloak; and after twisting some thorns into a
crown, they put it on him. [18]And they began saluting
him, "Hail, King of the Jews!" [19]They struck his head with
a reed, spat upon him, and knelt down in homage to
him. [20]After mocking him, they stripped him of the pur-
ple cloak and put his own clothes on him. Then they led
him out to crucify him.

Jesus' Illegal Trial

In the Jewish *Mishna,* a tract called "Sanhedrin" identifies a number of violations that prove Jesus' Sanhedrin trial was illegal:

(1) Trials were never to take place at night.

(2) Trials were never to take place on the eve of a Sabbath or festival day.

(3) A full day must be allowed to pass before a verdict of condemnation could be issued.

(4) The Sanhedrin could not meet in the high priest's palace.

(5) False witnesses could not be used. The penalty for this violation was execution.[2]

---

his manhood, named the baby, *Savior*. Shepherds and Wise Men brought gifts to celebrate the birth.

Thirty years later, the baby from Kerioth named Judas (*Praise*) and the baby from Bethlehem named Jesus (*Savior*) met, and Judas followed Jesus as the Messiah. Gradually, Judas realized Jesus was not going to be the revolutionary military leader he expected the Messiah to be, and he "went to the chief priests in order to betray him to them" (14:10).

Mark 14:43 describes the betrayal. Judas assumed Jesus would be in Gethsemane. The "crowd with swords and clubs" was made up of Sanhedrin members, temple police officers, and a deputized mob.

Since it was dark, the mob needed Judas to identify Jesus with a kiss, a traditional greeting of respect and intimacy. The grammatical construction indicates that Judas kissed Jesus repeatedly and effusively, making the betrayal all the more heinous (14:45). Today, couples name their sons James, John, Mark, or Luke, but no one names their son Judas. He planted the kiss of betrayal on the body of our Lord.

The calm self-control of Jesus during the last hours before the cross stands in sharp contrast to the frantic, turbulent behavior of those around him.

Today, the body of Christ is the church, and it's still possible for us to commit the same crime. When, like Judas, we fail to do our part, when our allegiance to the church is shallow, when we steal from the money that belongs to God, we too plant the kiss of betrayal on the "body of Christ."

Only Simon Peter (identified in John 18:10) made a vain attempt to defend Jesus by swinging his sword at the slave of the high priest. Peter is usually faulted for his violent outburst, but, unlike the other disciples, at least he demonstrated some courage. Peter has been condemned by some who would not venture a tenth part of what he ventured for his Lord.

Nevertheless, Jesus denounced the use of force, because

(1) Violence destroys those who employ it (Matthew 26:52).
(2) Jesus trusted his Father's ability to protect him (Matt. 26:53).

(3) Jesus recognized that his Father's will for him included suffering (Matt. 26:54).

During our Baptist denominational conflict, some have taken up worldly weapons such as precinct political strategies, coercion, and government entanglement to have their way. They may be repeating Peter's mistake with less excuse than he and with very little of either his courage or his love. Remember, Jesus warned us not to fight the kingdom's battles with worldly weapons. Paul repeated the same caution in 2 Corinthians 10:3–4, "Indeed, we live as human beings, but we do not wage war according to human standards; for the weapons of our warfare are not merely human, but they have divine power to destroy strongholds."

In contrast to Judas, Jesus remained loyal to the Father, following God's will in spite of the cost. Jesus is like an oasis of serenity in all the disordered scene. His is the calm assurance of one who knows he is following the will of God, and therefore has no reason to be afraid.

The High Priest (14:53–64)

According to Mark, the first of Jesus' two trials was before the Sanhedrin, the Jewish supreme court presided over by the high priest (Caiaphas, according to Matt. 26:57). Late at night the mob led Jesus to the meeting place within the temple precinct. Since the

Sanhedrin had limited power under Rome, this hearing was like a grand jury preparing a charge on which Jesus could be tried before the Roman governor.

Mark already told us they had been looking for a sly way to arrest and kill Jesus (Mk. 14:1). Now the council was looking for evidence against him. The law stated that at least two witnesses must agree before a sentence of death could be recommended. Of course, there were plenty of witnesses in Jerusalem who would testify, *this man healed me*, or *this man raised my daughter from the dead*, but that was not the evidence the council was looking for. So, they enlisted false witnesses. When the high priest realized their contrived testimonies were contradictory, he began to question Jesus directly (14:59–60).

When, like Judas, we fail to do our part, when our allegiance to the church is shallow, when we steal from the money that belongs to God, we too plant the kiss of betrayal on the "body of Christ."

Jesus made no response to the false witnesses. He did, however, answer Caiaphas' direct question (14:61), "Are you the Messiah, the Son of the Blessed One?"

"I am," Jesus responded (14:62), adding a quotation from Daniel 7:13 and Psalm 110:1, "You will see the Son of Man seated at the right hand of the Power . . . ."

What was blasphemous about Jesus' words? It was not his claim to be the Messiah and the "Son of the

Blessed," a term that David and others had used. Jesus was claiming to be more than that. He claimed to have divine authority at the right hand of God. He would be the final judge at the end of time, and they would one day see it. Such a claim to supernatural intimacy with "the Blessed One" was considered blasphemy. Even Jesus' term "I am" was a problem. "I am" was actually a reference to the name of God and was forbidden to be used (see Exodus 3:14).

Jesus' words were all the high priest needed. Tearing his clothing, a traditional signal of disgust, Caiaphas called for an immediate verdict from the council. The prescribed punishment for blasphemy was in Leviticus 24:16: "One who blasphemes the name of the Lord shall be put to death; the whole congregation shall stone the blasphemer." So, "all of them condemned him as deserving death" (Mk. 14:64).

. . . Jesus warned us not to fight the kingdom's battles with worldly weapons.

What a contrast. Here is the high priest, trying to please the Sanhedrin and curry the favor of the occupation government, trying to find an easy way out, wanting to get rid of Jesus, but happy to pass the responsibility for the whole mess into Pilate's hand. And here is Jesus, courageous, calm, and under control. Jesus knew an honest answer to the high priest's question meant death, and yet Jesus answered unhesitatingly. Jesus was confident that no matter what happened, if he trusted God, he would ultimately triumph.

Simon Peter (14:54, 66–72)

The Gospel of Mark is based on the eyewitness testimony of Simon Peter. It is remarkable, therefore, that Peter would include the embarrassing story of his own cowardly denial. Mark must have intertwined the story of Peter's denial with the trial of Jesus in order to warn Christians in Rome who would soon face persecution that even Peter, the prince of the apostles, denied Jesus. They might too if they were not spiritually prepared. In his preaching, Peter must have told the story over and over. *This is how I failed, but Jesus never stopped loving me. His grace forgave me. No matter what you've done, Jesus can forgive you and save you.*

Jesus is like an oasis of serenity in all the disordered scene.

When the servant girl accused Peter, she was expressing a popular contempt for Galileans from Nazareth. "You also were with Jesus, the man from Nazareth" (14:67). They told ethnic jokes about Nazarenes in the first century. No doubt everybody laughed when Nathaniel asked (John 1:46), "'Can anything good come out of Nazareth?'" The crowd understood when she accused Peter by association. Peter denied it once, twice, and three times.

But Peter's denial was an odd mixture of courage and cowardice. Remember, Peter had just attacked the high priest's servant. Good sense would suggest that he lie low, certainly not walk right into the courtyard of the high priest! Peter denied Jesus, but he was brave enough to follow Jesus—even at a distance.

Mark leaves us with some unanswered questions. Why didn't they arrest Peter? How did he escape? What did he do next? Obviously, Mark was not interested in merely relating the facts. He wanted to contrast the behavior of Peter and Jesus. David Garland points out that while Jesus was under fire inside, Peter warmed himself by the fire outside. While Jesus confessed under pressure inside and sealed his fate, Peter capitulated outside under gentle pressure and lied to save himself.[1] Both Peter and Jesus were on trial here. Peter failed his trial. Jesus triumphed in his.

Jesus was confident that no matter what happened, if he trusted God, he would ultimately triumph.

The Sanhedrin Mob (14:65)

Even some of the illustrious Sanhedrin judges joined the temple police and the mob in an outburst of crude horseplay: spitting on Jesus, callously ridiculing Jesus' claim to be a prophet, and beating him. Ironically, at the very time Jesus' prophecies about his arrest were coming true exactly as he predicted, his unbelieving enemies were blindfolding him and taunting him to prophesy.

Again in sharp contrast to the riotous mob, Jesus stood silent and patient. His meek submission was

How We Are Identified

The servant girl's accusations of Simon Peter suggest three ways people identify us (Mark 14:67–70). We are recognized:

- By the leader we follow ("You also were with Jesus, the man from Nazareth.")
- By the group with whom we associate ("This man is one of them.")
- By the language we speak ("You are a Galilean.")[3]

more than mere heroism. He was bearing all that sinners could hurl at him. Even though blindfolded, Jesus could see and identify each one who hit him. He pitied them. With infinite tenderness, Jesus was ready to forgive.

Pilate (15:1–15)

The second trial took place very early on Friday morning, after the illegal nighttime hearing before the Sanhedrin. Mark's reference to a "consultation" (15:1) by the judges before taking Jesus to Pilate may suggest an attempt to validate their unlawful meeting. Although the Jewish leaders wanted to get rid of Jesus, the Romans actually sentenced and killed him. The New Testament account is not an example of anti-Semitism. Everybody shared the blame—even Jesus' faithless disciples.

The official Sanhedrin charge was blasphemy, but that was not what they brought to Pilate. They charged Jesus with political violations: perverting the people, forbidding them to give tribute to Caesar, and calling himself a king (see Luke 23:1–5).

They and Pilate knew it was a lie. Jesus' answer, "You say so" (Mk. 15:2), implied, *I have claimed to be the king of the Jews, but you know very well that the interpretation my accusers are putting on that claim is not my interpretation. I am no political revolutionary. My kingdom is a spiritual kingdom of love.*

Thinking he could play the crowd against the chief priests, Pilate offered them a choice between releasing a revolutionary murderer named Barabbas or releasing Jesus. Matthew identified Barabbas as Jesus Barabbas (Matt. 27:16). The name Barabbas means *son of a father*, and so the choice was between *Jesus, son of a father* and *Jesus, the true Son of the Father*. The Sanhedrin incited the crowd to choose Barabbas and call for the crucifixion of Jesus.

Once again, Mark draws a contrast—this time between the behavior of Jesus and Pilate. Pilate knew the unjust nature of the charges. He even received a divine warning in a dream (Matt. 27:19). So it was really Pilate on trial in Jerusalem, not Jesus. Pilate chose political expediency over justice. We do the same whenever we follow the choices of least resistance and when we take a position because it's popular, even though we know someone is suffering unjustly.

During the recent denominational conflict, it was painful to hear a Baptist preacher say, "I voted with them because they helped me get a church," or to watch some church leaders go along with the majority in order to be on the winning side.

The Roman Soldiers (15:16–20)

The "governor's headquarters" (Mk. 15:16) was any place where a high Roman official conducted affairs. The traditional site of the soldier's mockery is the Fortress Antonia adjoining the northwest corner of the temple compound. Visitors today can see a stone pavement where Roman soldiers carved board games and other trivia. The location may have been there, but more likely Pilate would be residing in luxury at the palace of Herod the Great, not in the sparse military barracks.

. . . Jesus teaches us how to endure suffering with peace and grace, trusting in God to deliver us.

The "whole cohort" (15:16) could be from 400 to 600 soldiers. All of them joined in the mockery. They put a purple cloth on Jesus and crowned him with a tiara fashioned from a thorny bush in order to mock Jesus' claim to be king. Striking Jesus with a reed, they bowed down in comic homage before leading him to the place of execution.

It's interesting to notice Mark's change in grammar in this account. Earlier, Mark had presented Jesus as the actor, the initiator who dramatically changed things—sickness, storms, hunger, cruelty, and even death. But now, Jesus was passive. In this passage we are studying, Jesus is the subject of only nine verbs and the object of fifty-six. In contrast to those around him, Jesus teaches us how to endure suffering with peace and grace, trusting in God to deliver us.

We are the ones on trial, not Jesus.

Following Jesus' Example

Mark shows us the example of Jesus. Mark also warns us that we can become a jealous Judas, a cunning Caiaphas, a paradoxical Peter, a pretentious Pilate, a mindless member of a hate-filled mob, a sordid soldier, or a defeated disciple hiding in fear. We are the ones on trial, not Jesus.

QUESTIONS

1. Who is really to blame for the death of Jesus—the Jewish leaders, the Roman authorities, the mob? Or was it merely God's plan?

2. Do circumstances excuse the conduct of Judas, Peter, Pilate, the disciples, the others?

3. When we meet unexpected crises, how can the example of Jesus help us?

4. Who are some other personalities in the Bible who remained faithful and calm when their faith was challenged?

NOTES

1. David E. Garland, *Mark*, The NIV Application Commentary (Grand Rapids, Michigan: Zondervan Publishing House, 1996), 566.
2. See James A. Brooks, *Mark*, The New American Commentary, vol. 23 (Nashville: Broadman Press, 1991), 240.
3. David McKenna, *Mark*, The Communicator's Commentary (Waco, Texas: Word Books, Publisher, 1985), 304.

Focal Text

Mark 15:21–41; 16:1–8

Background

Mark 15:21—16:8

Main Idea

Jesus' crucifixion and resurrection show that Jesus was truly God's Son.

Question to Explore

What elements in Jesus' life, death, and resurrection lead to belief in him?

LESSON THIRTEEN

Jesus Dies and Lives Again!

Study Aim

To identify elements in Jesus' ministry, crucifixion, and resurrection that show that Jesus was truly God's Son who deserves our commitment of life

Study and Action Emphases

- Share the gospel of Jesus Christ with all people
- Equip people for ministry in the church and in the world
- Strengthen existing churches and start new congregations

Quick Read

Jesus gave his life on the cross, completing his Father's plan. Jesus' resurrection validates his ministry, proving that Jesus is indeed the Son of God and the Savior of the world.

The earliest Christians didn't celebrate Christmas, but every week they set aside a day to commemorate the death and resurrection of Jesus. These two themes were like a fire at the heart of the gospel, blazing as the main subject of the New Testament.

The Crucifixion of Jesus (15:21–41)

1. *Simon of Cyrene carries the cross (15:21).* The routine procedures of Roman crucifixion seldom varied. A two-piece wooden cross would be recycled or else constructed in a government-subsidized carpenter shop. The condemned criminal had to carry the heavy cross beam to the place of execution, walking in the middle of four soldiers. A fifth soldier carried a placard specifying the felon's crimes. They took the longest possible route, exposing the frightening spectacle to as many viewers as possible. Then they secured the hands of the condemned to the wooden cross beam, hoisted the condemned criminal, and fastened the wooden cross beam to the upright beam, which was already embedded in the ground. After anchoring his feet to the upright beam, they left the victim to die from pain, exposure, asphyxiation, muscle fatigue, and exposure. Death usually took several days.

Weakened from the brutal flogging and from lack of sleep and food, Jesus apparently fell under the load of the cross. The centurion quickly scouted the crowd and drafted Simon of Cyrene to carry the cross to

Mark 15:21–41

21 They compelled a passer-by, who was coming in from
the country, to carry his cross; it was Simon of Cyrene,
the father of Alexander and Rufus. 22 Then they brought
Jesus to the place called Golgotha (which means the
place of a skull). 23 And they offered him wine mixed with
myrrh; but he did not take it. 24 And they crucified him,
and divided his clothes among them, casting lots to
decide what each should take.

25 It was nine o'clock in the morning when they cruci-
fied him. 26 The inscription of the charge against him
read, "The King of the Jews." 27 And with him they cruci-
fied two bandits, one on his right and one on his left.
29 Those who passed by derided him, shaking their heads
and saying, "Aha! You who would destroy the temple
and build it in three days, 30 save yourself, and come
down from the cross!" 31 In the same way the chief
priests, along with the scribes, were also mocking him
among themselves and saying, "He saved others; he can-
not save himself. 32 Let the Messiah, the King of Israel,
come down from the cross now, so that we may see and
believe." Those who were crucified with him also
taunted him.

33 When it was noon, darkness came over the whole
land until three in the afternoon. 34 At three o'clock Jesus
cried out with a loud voice, "Eloi, Eloi, lema
sabachthani?" which means, "My God, my God, why
have you forsaken me?" 35 When some of the bystanders

heard it, they said, "Listen, he is calling for Elijah." 36And
someone ran, filled a sponge with sour wine, put it on a
stick, and gave it to him to drink, saying, "Wait, let us see
whether Elijah will come to take him down." 37Then Jesus
gave a loud cry and breathed his last. 38And the curtain of
the temple was torn in two, from top to bottom. 39Now
when the centurion, who stood facing him, saw that in
this way he breathed his last, he said, "Truly this man
was God's Son!"

40There were also women looking on from a distance;
among them were Mary Magdalene, and Mary the
mother of James the younger and of Joses, and Salome.
41These used to follow him and provided for him when
he was in Galilee; and there were many other women
who had come up with him to Jerusalem.

Mark 16:1–8

1When the sabbath was over, Mary Magdalene, and
Mary the mother of James, and Salome bought spices, so
that they might go and anoint him. 2And very early on
the first day of the week, when the sun had risen, they
went to the tomb. 3They had been saying to one
another, "Who will roll away the stone for us from the
entrance to the tomb?" 4When they looked up, they saw
that the stone, which was very large, had already been
rolled back. 5As they entered the tomb, they saw a young
man, dressed in a white robe, sitting on the right side;
and they were alarmed. 6But he said to them, "Do not be

alarmed; you are looking for Jesus of Nazareth, who was crucified. He has been raised; he is not here. Look, there is the place they laid him. [7]But go, tell his disciples and Peter that he is going ahead of you to Galilee; there you will see him, just as he told you." [8]So they went out and fled from the tomb, for terror and amazement had seized them; and they said nothing to anyone, for they were afraid.

Golgotha. Simon, probably a proselyte Jew, was in Jerusalem to observe the Passover (see Acts 2:10 for a reference to people from Cyrene in Jerusalem).

Shouldering the cross must have been a grim, revolting experience, like fingering a hangman's noose. Providentially, however, this experience became the most important incident in Simon's life. At some point, Simon came to believe that Jesus was the Messiah. What evidence do we have of this?

Mark's Gospel was written for Christians in the church in Rome. He alone identified Simon as the father of Alexander and Rufus, who must have been recognized by the readers as prominent leaders in their congregation (Mark 15:21). Later, when Paul concluded a letter to this same Roman church, he wrote, "Greet Rufus, chosen in the Lord; and greet his mother—a mother to me also" (Romans 16:13). Probably this Rufus was Simon's son, and Rufus's mother was Simon's wife. Furthermore, in Acts 13:1, among the leaders of the church in Antioch are

"Simon who was called Niger" and Lucius from Cyrene. It's probable that Simon of Cyrene not only became a believer who led his own wife and sons to Christ but also became a missionary helping to spread the gospel to Antioch.

2. *Soldiers carry out the execution (15:22–27).* Mark's account is characterized by brevity, reverence, and restraint. His main purpose was to reinforce the

Jesus Christ—Lord of All

According to Mark, Jesus' death and resurrection fulfilled Old Testament prophecy. Obviously first century Christians read Scripture in the light of their experience with the Lord. Jesus was the criterion by which they interpreted the Bible.

That's why so many Baptists were upset when revisers of the 1963 edition of *The Baptist Faith and Message* recently deleted the statement: "The criterion by which the Bible is to be interpreted is Jesus Christ." Baptists have long believed that the Bible is a book of faith and cannot be fully understood from the outside by grammar and history alone. It must be understood from its center—Jesus Christ—who said, "The Scriptures . . . testify on my behalf" (John 5:39).

The Bible, therefore, is best understood by believers who read it in the light of their personal relationship with the Lord. Through Jesus as the criterion or standard, the Bible becomes unified and consistent. To delete this Christological criterion weakens the idea that Jesus Christ is the Lord of the Bible, and contradicts what Mark and other inspired New Testament writers have taught us.

conviction of early believers that Jesus was the Son of God just as Jesus claimed. Mark did not dwell, as some do today, on the details of Jesus' physical suffering, but instead showed how everything that happened was in fulfillment of Old Testament prophecy, particularly Psalm 22. To these early believers, Jesus was the criterion by which they interpreted the Old Testament Scriptures.

It's probable that Simon of Cyrene not only became a believer who led his own wife and sons to Christ but also became a missionary helping to spread the gospel to Antioch.

Golgotha is an Aramaic word meaning "skull." None of the gospels locates the place, but we do know that such executions were held outside city walls and along public roads. The term Golgotha (meaning "skull") might have been a posted warning to travelers of some danger along a road, like the "skull and crossbones" symbol warns of danger today.

Since AD 326, the traditional location of Golgotha has been occupied by the Church of the Holy Sepulcher. This claim was reinforced by recent archeological discoveries proving that in the first century, it would have stood outside the wall on the northwest side of Jerusalem. Another location called Gordon's Calvary and the adjacent Garden Tomb just outside the Damascus Gate is also a popular site for tourists. But the tomb in that location is from a much later time than the time of Jesus.

Wine mixed with myrrh (15:23) was a narcotic combination offered to the dying victims to deaden their pain. Jesus refused it so he could face death in complete control.

Since clothing was a valuable commodity in the first century, the executioners were customarily allowed to confiscate the condemned man's clothing. For Jesus, it was one more humiliation to have his clothing raffled off at the foot of the cross (15:24).

It is precisely because Jesus did not come down from the cross that we believe in him.

According to Mark's chronology, Jesus was crucified at 9 a.m. Darkness covered the land at 12 noon, and Jesus cried with a loud voice and died at 3 p.m. The timing of the crucifixion is different from John 19:14. We must remember that both Mark and John were less concerned about logical order than about theological meaning.

Note Mark 15:26. Customarily, the charges against the condemned were posted on the cross. In Jesus' case the inscription was, "'The King of the Jews.'" The words were intended to be a sarcastic insult, but the placard told the truth unwittingly.

The two bandits crucified on either side of Jesus (15:27) were probably rebels, maybe two of the insurrectionists mentioned in 15:7. Mark may have intentionally added the detail, "one on his right and one on his left," to remind readers of the request of James and John in 10:37. Being crucified with Jesus is what occupying places of "honor" in the kingdom really means.

As was often his style, Mark emphasized certain ironic contrasts in the story. For example, Simon the apostle denied Jesus and hid, while Simon the stranger carried Jesus' cross. James and John, who said they wanted to be at Jesus' side, were absent, while two bandits took their places.

3. *The crowd carries on the mockery (15:29–32).* A voyeuristic crowd "shaking their heads" (15:29) made fun of Jesus. Joining them in a more sophisticated ridicule were the chief priests and scribes who sarcastically challenged Jesus' claim to be a king. They all dared Jesus to perform another miracle, come down from the cross, and save himself. Little did they know that Jesus could have done it, but would not so he could offer them salvation. It is precisely because Jesus did not come down from the cross that we believe in him.

4. *Jesus carries the sins of the world (15:33–39).* To convince readers that Jesus was the Son of God, Mark emphasized Jesus' divine-human nature. As God, Jesus was in control, fulfilling prophecy, forgiving sins. As man, Jesus was tired, bled, and was thirsty and even perplexed, asking, "'Why have you forsaken me?'"

The supernatural occurrences accompanying the death of Jesus were vindications of Jesus' claim to be the Son of God. Some have tried to explain the darkness in verse 33 as an eclipse, a dust storm, or heavy rain clouds. But Mark implies no such natural explanation, content instead to report it as a mysterious miraculous sign.

The last words of Jesus from the cross (15:34) show his death was an atoning sacrifice for the sins of the world. The mysterious Aramaic words of abandonment reveal the depth of Jesus' suffering. The ultimate punishment for sin is to be separated from God, and Jesus was experiencing that separation on behalf of all sinners. As Paul put it, "For our sake he made him to be sin who knew no sin, so that in him we might become the righteousness of God" (2 Corinthians 5:21).

Most crucified victims became weaker and weaker until they slowly expired. But Mark indicates that while Jesus was still strong, he died suddenly and violently, with "a loud cry" (Mark 15:37), suggesting that Jesus' death was a willful act of victory.

The supernatural occurrences accompanying the death of Jesus were vindications of Jesus' claim to be the Son of God.

Another mysterious miracle proving the authenticity of Jesus' messiahship was the tearing of the temple curtain (15:38). This occurrence was a preview of the future destruction of the temple, the termination of the old sacrificial system, and the opening up of access to God to all who believe in Jesus.

The Roman in charge of the crucifixion (tradition names him Longinus) was no doubt a campaign-hardened foot soldier who had seen many men die. He likely had witnessed previous crucifixions, but this time he saw something different. Impressed with the conduct of Jesus as Jesus died, and somehow being familiar with Jewish theology, the centurion came to believe that Jesus was the Messiah, the Son of God (15:39). Mark may be suggesting that the centurion represented future Gentiles who would believe in Jesus.

5. *The women carry on faithfully (15:40–41).* Mary from Magdala on the shore of Galilee was the one from whom Jesus had cast out seven demons (Luke 8:2). Mary the mother of James the younger and Joses is sometimes identified as the mother of Jesus, because Jesus had brothers named James and Joses (Mark 6:3). It is true that Jesus' mother was at the cross (John 19:26), but it seems odd that Mark would refer to the mother of the Lord in this way. Others identify this Mary with the wife of Clopas in John 19:25. Salome was the mother of James and John (Matthew 27:56) and perhaps was the sister of Jesus' mother (John 19:25).

This faithful trio, along with "many other women" (Mark 15:40), had "provided for him when he was in Galilee" (15:40). They also provided the eyewitness accounts of the crucifixion, burial, and resurrection of Jesus.

The Resurrection of Jesus (15:42—16:8)

1. *Jesus dead and buried (15:42–47).* Why would the Bible give so much detailed attention to the burial of Jesus, even including it in early statements of faith?

For example, 1 Corinthians 15:3–5 states "that Christ died for our sins in accordance with the scriptures, and that he was buried, and that he was raised on the third day in accordance with the scriptures." Why this attention to the burial?

For one thing, the burial proved that Jesus really died and that he didn't just faint and then later awaken as some skeptics taught. Also, the details made it certain that the empty tomb was the same one in which Jesus was buried and that the women didn't make a location error and mistakenly report Jesus' body missing. Later, people who were known as Gnostics taught that Jesus switched places with Simon of Cyrene. So when Simon carried the cross to Golgotha, the soldiers were confused and crucified him, while Jesus slipped away in the crowd and remained alive. The detailed attention given to the burial was an intentional effort to counter such false claims.

The ultimate punishment for sin is to be separated from God, and Jesus was experiencing that separation on behalf of all sinners.

Not much is known of Joseph of Arimathea, and the location of Arimathea is not clear. As a member of the Sanhedrin, he may have been the one who gave Mark the details of the trial. According to Mark, he was "respected," was "waiting expectantly for the kingdom of God," and was courageous (15:42). Luke 23:50–51 indicates he did not agree with the decision of the Sanhedrin.

The Resurrection

The resurrection has a three-dimensional application:

- *The Past—Jesus arose.* We can accept the facts: Sunday morning, two women discovered the tomb open and empty (Mark 16:6).
- *The Present—Jesus is alive.* "He is going ahead of you . . . . You will see him" (16:7). Because Jesus lives, we not only know about him; we can know Jesus, walking and talking with him daily.
- *The Future—Jesus will raise us from the dead.* Paul and others explained what Mark's resurrection story means to us. We can be sure "the one who raised the Lord Jesus will raise us also with Jesus" (2 Corinthians 4:14).

Because death by crucifixion usually took several days, Pilate was surprised that after only six hours Jesus was already dead. Pilate called the centurion to verify Jesus' death. Being wealthy, Joseph purchased the burial necessities and probably had servants who helped him prepare the body. (John 19:38–39 states that Nicodemus assisted him.) Ancient Jews seldom buried in the ground but used a natural cave or, as here, hollowed out a cavity in a cliff. Jewish custom was to use a stone to close the opening to keep out animals or grave robbers.

2. *Jesus alive and raised (16:1–8).* The ending of Mark's Gospel has long been disputed. This debate

highlights the contribution of linguistic scholars who continually work at determining the most accurate Greek text on which to base our English translations. Even the most conservative students of the Bible believe that verses 9 through 20 were not in Mark's original writing, and that the Gospel of Mark should end with verse 8. (My dad, a deacon at First Baptist Church, Dallas, Texas, told me how pastor W. A. Criswell one day declared from the pulpit, "You should take scissors and cut out these last verses, because they don't belong in the Word of God!")

The last words of Jesus from the cross (15:34) show his death was an atoning sacrifice for the sins of the world.

The first eight verses, however, are enough. They give us a clear and certain declaration of the central truth of our Christian faith, that Jesus Christ rose from the dead and is alive today. Early on Sunday, the two Marys went to the tomb of Joseph to anoint Jesus' corpse. Worried about the heavy stone, they were surprised to find it already removed. Jesus' body was gone, but an angelic being in a white robe, who was specifically sitting on the right side of the tomb, told them Jesus had been raised from the dead. The angel sent them back to tell the good news. Apparently, out of fear, they were reluctant to speak at first. But obviously they eventually obeyed, otherwise Mark would not have known these details.

Mark leaves to others the task of reporting the appearances and the excitement of the disciples. His abrupt ending may be his way of showing that the story was not complete, only just beginning. Perhaps he wanted the readers to continue the story in their own lives and pass it on.

To convince readers that Jesus was the Son of God, Mark emphasized Jesus' divine-human nature.

Mark began his gospel with the messenger of God telling what God was going to do (Mark 1:2–8). Mark now ends his gospel with the messenger of God telling what God has done.

QUESTIONS

1. What are some evidences from the first century that Jesus rose from the dead?
2. Mark describes how Simon carried the cross of Christ. What does it mean for us to take up our cross and follow Jesus?
3. How are both the deity and humanity of Jesus revealed in this lesson?
4. What was the curtain in the temple (15:38), and what was the significance of its being torn from top to bottom?
5. How did Mark learn about the details of the secret, nighttime trial of Jesus before the Sanhedrin? How did he learn about the details of the crucifixion and resurrection?

Our Next New Study

(Available for use June 2002)

Hebrews and James

HEBREWS: GOD'S MESSAGE TO HALFHEARTED CHRISTIANS

Lesson 1	Pay Closer Attention to God's Message	Hebrews 1:1–4; 2:1–11, 14–18
Lesson 2	Heed God's Call to Obedient Faith	Hebrews 3:1–6, 12—4:1, 6–13
Lesson 3	Press On to Maturity	Hebrews 4:14–16; 5:11—6:12
Lesson 4	Remember Who Jesus Is	Hebrews 7:11–17, 26—8:13
Lesson 5	Live in a New Relationship with God	Hebrews 9:11–15, 24—10:4, 19–25
Lesson 6	Be Faithful to God No Matter What	Hebrews 11:1–2, 8–22, 39—12:3, 12–13
Lesson 7	Do Not Refuse the One Who Is Speaking	Hebrews12:25—13:8, 20–21

JAMES: HOW REAL FAITH ACTS

Lesson 8	Faith Reaching Toward Maturity	James 1:2–8, 11–15, 22–27
Lesson 9	How to Tell When Your Faith Is Real	James 2:1–19
Lesson 10	Watch What You Say	James 3:1–12
Lesson 11	Stop Quarreling	James 4:1–12
Lesson 12	Foolish Living	James 4:13—5:6
Lesson 13	What Church Ought to Be Like	James 5:7–20

Additional Resources for Studying *Hebrews*[1]

F.F. Bruce. *The Epistle to the Hebrews.* The New International Commentary on the New Testament. Revised edition. Grand Rapids, Michigan: William B. Eerdmans Publishing Company, 1990.

Fred B. Craddock. "The Letter to the Hebrews." *The New Interpreter's Bible.* Volume XII. Nashville: Abingdon Press, 1998.

Robert J. Dean. *Hebrews: Call to Christian Commitment.* Nashville, Tennessee: Convention Press, 1985.

William G. Johnsson. *Hebrews.* Knox Preaching Guides. Atlanta: John Knox Press, 1980.

William L. Lane, *Hebrews 1—8.* Word Biblical Commentary. Volume 47a. Dallas, Texas: Word Books, Publisher, 1991.

William L. Lane. *Hebrews 9–13.* Word Biblical Commentary. Volume 47b. Dallas, Texas: Word Books, Publisher, 1991.

Thomas G. Long. *Hebrews*. Interpretation: A Bible Commentary for Teaching and Preaching. Louisville: John Knox Press, 1997.

A.T. Robertson. *Word Pictures in the New Testament*. Volume V. Nashville, Tennessee: Broadman Press, 1932.

Additional Resources for Studying James

Luke Timothy Johnson. "James." *The New Interpreter's Bible*. Volume XII. Nashville: Abingdon Press, 1998.

Ralph P. Martin. *James*. Word Biblical Commentary. Volume 48. Dallas, Texas: Word Books, Publisher, 1988.

A.T. Robertson. *Word Pictures in the New Testament*. Volume VI. Nashville, Tennessee: Broadman Press, 1933.

Harold S. Songer. "James." *The Broadman Bible Commentary*. Volume 12. Nashville, Tennessee: Broadman Press, 1972.

NOTES

1. Listing a book does not imply full agreement by the writers or BAPTISTWAY PRESS® with all of its comments.

How to Order More Bible Study Materials

It's easy! Just fill in the following information. (Note: when the *Teaching Guide* is priced at $2.45, the *Teaching Guide* includes Bible comments for teachers.)

Title of item	Price	Quantity	Cost
This Issue			
Jesus in the Gospel of Mark—Study Guide	$1.95	______	______
Jesus in the Gospel of Mark—Large Print Study Guide	$1.95	______	______
Jesus in the Gospel of Mark—Teaching Guide	$2.45	______	______
Previous Issues Available:			
God's Message in the Old Testament—Study Guide	$1.95	______	______
God's Message in the Old Testament—Teaching Guide	$1.95	______	______
Genesis 12—50: Family Matters—Study Guide	$1.95	______	______
Genesis 12—50: Family Matters—Large Print Study Guide	$1.95	______	______
Genesis 12—50: Family Matters—Teaching Guide	$2.45	______	______
Good News in the New Testament—Study Guide	$1.95	______	______
Good News in the New Testament—Large Print Study Guide	$1.95	______	______
Good News in the New Testament—Teaching Guide	$2.45	______	______
Matthew: Jesus As the Fulfillment of God's Promises—Study Guide	$1.95	______	______
Matthew: Jesus As the Fulfillment of God's Promises—Large Print Study Guide	$1.95	______	______
Matthew: Jesus As the Fulfillment of God's Promises—Teaching Guide	$2.45	______	______
Acts: Sharing God's Good News with Everyone—Study Guide	$1.95	______	______
Acts: Sharing God's Good News with Everyone —Teaching Guide	$1.95	______	______
Romans: Good News for a Troubled World—Study Guide	$1.95	______	______
Romans: Good News for a Troubled World—Teaching Guide	$1.95	______	______
Galatians: By Grace Through Faith, and Ephesians: God's Plan and Our Response—Study Guide	$1.95	______	______
Galatians: By Grace Through Faith, and Ephesians: God's Plan and Our Response—Large Print Study Guide	$1.95	______	______
Galatians: By Grace Through Faith, and Ephesians: God's Plan and Our Response—Teaching Guide	$2.45	______	______
Coming for use beginning June 2002			
Hebrews and James—Study Guide	$1.95	______	______
Hebrews and James—Large Print Study Guide	$1.95	______	______
Hebrews and James—Teaching Guide	$2.45	______	______
Coming for use beginning September 2002			
1 Corinthians—Study Guide	$1.95	______	______
1 Corinthians —Large Print Study Guide	$1.95	______	______
1 Corinthians —Teaching Guide	$2.45	______	______

Beliefs Important to Baptists

Who in the World Are Baptists, Anyway? (one lesson)	$ .45	________	________
Who in the World Are Baptists, Anyway?—Teacher's Edition	$ .55	________	________
Beliefs Important to Baptists: I (four lessons)	$1.35	________	________
Beliefs Important to Baptists: I—Teacher's Edition	$1.75	________	________
Beliefs Important to Baptists: II (four lessons)	$1.35	________	________
Beliefs Important to Baptists: II—Teacher's Edition	$1.75	________	________
Beliefs Important to Baptists: III (four lessons)	$1.35	________	________
Beliefs Important to Baptists: III—Teacher's Edition	$1.75	________	________

*Charges for standard shipping service:

Subtotal up to $20.00	$3.95
Subtotal $20.01—$50.00	$4.95
Subtotal $50.01—$100.00	10% of subtotal
Subtotal $100.01 and up	8% of subtotal

Please allow three weeks for standard delivery. For express shipping service: Call 1-866-249-1799 for information on additional charges.

Subtotal ____________

Shipping* ____________

TOTAL ____________

Number of FREE copies of *Brief Basics for Texas Baptists* needed for leading adult Sunday School department periods ____

____
Your name

____
Your church

____
Mailing address

____
City State Zip code

MAIL this form with your check for the total amount to
Bible Study/Discipleship Center
Baptist General Convention of Texas
333 North Washington
Dallas, TX 75246-1798
(Make checks to "Baptist Executive Board.")

OR, **FAX** your order anytime to: 214-828-5187, and we will bill you.

OR, **CALL** your order toll-free: 1-866-249-1799
(8:30 a.m.-5:00 p.m., M-F), and we will bill you.

OR, **E-MAIL** your order to our internet e-mail address:
baptistway@bgct.org, and we will bill you.
We look forward to receiving your order! Thank you!